C000255492

PLACE

YORKSHIRE

The Yorkshire Dales

The North York Moors

The Yorkshire Wolds

Pennine Yorkshire

Brontë Country

The Yorkshire Coast

York • Leeds • Bradford

Sheffield • Wakefield • Hull

Keith & Chris Hendry

PLACES OF INTEREST

First Published in March 2003 by Keith and Chris Hendry, Heath House, Moor Road, Knayton, Thirsk, YO7 4AZ.
Tel. 07831 223 437

E-mail rkhendry@aol.com

Copyright © Keith and Chris Hendry 2003

ISBN: 0-9544531-0-7

Publisher's Note

The cover picture is by kind permission of the Bolton Abbey Estate and the logos by kind permission of Roam'in Tours of York and York Maize Maze.

Pictures associated with named PLACES have been supplied by the respective owners. Other pictures are by the authors.

Printed by G. H. Smith & Son, Easingwold, York.

CONTENTS

AN INTRODUCTION TO YORKSHIRE

Yorkshire is host to two National Parks, the **Yorkshire Dales** (p5) and the **North York Moors** (p5) as well as the rolling **Yorkshire Wolds** (p6), heather-clad **Pennine Yorkshire** (p7), the rugged **Yorkshire Coast** (p7), great cities like **York** (p122), **Leeds** (p64), **Bradford** (p26) and **Sheffield** (p110), long established market towns like **Skipton** (p112) and **Ingleton** (p60) and hundreds of abbeys, castles, great houses, gardens, museums and places of historic, archaeological or scenic interest all framed by high moors, wooded hills and lush farming country.

Yorkshire's grandeur has inspired the Brontës of **Haworth** (p49), the sculptor **Henry Moore** (p65) the artist **David Hockney** (p32), superb choirs and the world's best brass bands. All with their own vision.

Yorkshire vision changed the world. Captain Cook learned his skills at **Whitby** (p120) and sailed round the world in a flat bottomed Yorkshire collier boat. William Wilberforce set out from **Hull** (p55) to abolish slavery. The South Pennines was the birthplace of the Industrial Revolution and the might of our industry made Britain a world power. **York**, (p122) Roman stronghold and Viking capital, is one of Europe's greatest mediaeval cities.

The Northern part of the area covered by this book is made up largely of agricultural land and moors stretching from the **Yorkshire Dales** (p5) in the West across the fertile Hambleton and Harrogate Districts to the **North York Moors** (p5).

The central belt extends from the **Brontë Country** (p6) in the West across the Bradford, Leeds, York and Selby Districts to the rolling **Yorkshire Wolds** (p6) in the East.

The South of the county extends from **Pennine Yorkshire** (p7) in the West across the more populated South Yorkshire areas of Wakefield and Sheffield Districts.

Finally, fringing the Eastern strip from Captain Cook's country around Whitby all the way to Spurn Head, there is the timeless **Yorkshire Coast** (p7).

Try the Yorkshire Tourist Board site at

www.ytb.org.uk or **www.yorkshirevisitor.com**

The Yorkshire Dales.

This area is a rich mosaic of flower-filled meadows, high fells, heather moors and broad-leaved woodland, scattered with stone barns, drystone walls, an abundance of waterfalls and a rich heritage around every corner. It is a quiet, peaceful and unspoilt place in which to relax and unwind. The 'All Creatures Great and Small' scenery will impress just as much as James Herriot's stories.

Cradled in the valley bottoms, stone-built villages guard centuries of history. In these rural communities farming plays a vital role in maintaining the area's economy.

The Dales is a region with a rich and colourful tradition of arts, entertainment and celebration. Summer shows or galas, traditional sporting events, music, drama or an art exhibition, there is always something to inspire visitors of all ages.

The area is easily accessed by road on the West from the M6 and from the East by the A1. Cross Pennine routes include the M62, A59, A65 and A66 and many minor roads.

There are **Tourist Information Centres** at Aysgarth, Grassington, Hawes, Horton-in-Ribblesdale, Ingleton, Leyburn, Malham, Reeth, Richmond, Sedbergh, Settle and Skipton. See p8 for full details.

Try these useful sites
www.yorkshiredales.org   **www.ytb.org.uk**

The North York Moors.

A sense of space and solitude marks the North York Moors, where ridge upon ridge of heather moorland rolls into the purple distance. The deep secret valleys, which cut the plateau, come almost as a surprise and the warmth of their dreaming red-roofed villages gives pleasing contrast to the upland solitude.

Discover the grandeur of stately homes and the majestic ruins of abbeys and castles. There are market towns steeped in tradition which have remained unspoiled through generations. The villages of the moors are like stepping back in time with their beautiful architecture and warm hospitality.

There are **Tourist Information Centres** at Danby, Helmsley, Malton, Pickering and Sutton Bank. See p8 for full details.

Try these useful sites
www.moors.uk.net   www.ryedale.gov.uk
www.ytb.org

Brontë Country

The name comes from the three Brontë sisters whose novels and poems immortalised the austere moorlands which surrounded their home, now the **Brontë Parsonage Museum** (p50). It is an area of outstanding natural beauty with a diversity of landscape ranging from the serene to the wild and dramatic. It offers the moody solitude of the moorland hills and Pennines with the rural softness of the Yorkshire Dales, and provides the perfect base from which to experience its many attractions along with those adjoining the area.

There is a **Tourist Information Centre** at Haworth. See p8 for full details.

Try these useful sites
www.visitbrontecountry.com   www.bradford.gov.uk
www.ytb.org

Yorkshire Wolds.

Magnificent scenery in a countryside of unrivalled beauty and varied heritage await you. The Wolds are an outstanding and unspoilt holiday destination to which visitors return year after year.

Whether your ideal involves 'getting away from it all' or discovering fascinating local culture and heritage, you can be sure you will experience a visit to remember.

From the gentle undulating Yorkshire Wolds to the flat Holderness plain, the countryside is spectacular. Open roads lead to charming and ancient market towns with lovingly preserved old streets and buildings.

The Wolds have countless villages, with ancient inns, ponds and fine churches.

There is a **Tourist Information Centre** at Beverley. See p8 for full details.

Try these useful sites

www.east-riding-of-yorkshire.gov.uk
www.ryedale.gov.uk www.ytb.org

Pennine Yorkshire.

Encompasses the districts of Calderdale, Kirklees and Barnsley, a unique mix of hills and heritage, and town and country in a great location. That special sweep of high country from the Peak District to **Brontë Country** (p6) gives endless opportunities for walking, riding and cycling, in a landscape full of history and surprises.

Chances are you will recognise Pennine Yorkshire as the setting for "Last of the Summer Wine", "Where The Heart Is", "Brassed Off" and "Fanny and Elvis". The moving image dominates, but through the writing of the Brontës and Ted Hughes the power of the pen has made Pennine Yorkshire one of the world's great literary landscapes.

Although wild country this is no wilderness. Traditional and "alternative" towns and villages offer a countryside base with city attractions in easy reach. Excellent public transport makes exploring easy and kinder to the environment. You simply won't find a better touring base.

There are **Tourist Information Centres** at Barnsley, Batley, Halifax, Hebden Bridge, Holmfirth, Huddersfield and Todmorden, See p8 for full details.

Try these useful sites

www.pennineyorkshire.co.uk www.barnsley.gov.uk
www.calderdale.gov.uk www.kirklees.gov.uk
www.ytb.org

The Yorkshire Coast.

The Yorkshire Coast resorts are still as popular now as they were in their Victorian heyday. Esplanades and fine, manicured gardens are home to a varied programme of entertainment. There are safe sandy beaches, traditional fishing harbours, lively amusements and visitor attractions.

There are **Tourist Information Centre** at Bridlington, Filey, Hornsea, Scarborough, Whitby and Withernsea. See p8 for full details.

Try these useful sites

www.east-riding-of-yorkshire.gov.uk www.ytb.org

NATIONAL PARK CENTRES AND TOURIST INFORMATION CENTRES

Aysgarth Tel: 01969 663 424
Aysgarth Falls National Park Centre, Aysgarth Falls,
Leyburn, North Yorkshire, DL8 3TH
E-mail/www: aysgarth@ytbtic.co.uk
www.yorkshiredales.org www.destinationdales.org

Barnsley Tel: 01226 206 757
46, Eldon Street, Barnsley, S70 2JL
E-mail/www: barnsley@ytbtic.co.uk
www.barnsley.gov.uk

Batley Tel: 01924 423 172
Yorkshire Mill Village, Bradford Road, Batley, West
Yorkshire, WF17 5LZ
E-mail/www: batley@ytbtic.co.uk

Bedale Tel: 01677 424 604
Bedale Hall, Bedale, North Yorkshire, DL8 1AA
E-mail/www: bedale@ytbtic.co.uk
www.hambleton.gov.uk www.herriotcountry.com

Beverley Tel: 01482 867 430
34 Butcher Row, Beverley, East Riding of Yorkshire,
HU17 0AB
E-mail/www: beverley@ytbtic.co.uk
www.inbeverley.co.uk www.eastriding.gov.uk

Boroughbridge Tel: 01423 323 373
2 Fishergate, Boroughbridge. North Yorkshire, YO51
9AL
E-mail/www: www.harrogate.gov.uk/tourism

Bradford Tel: 01274 753 678
City Hall, Centenary Square, Bradford, BD1 1HY
E-mail/www: tourist.information@bradford.gov.uk
www.visitbradford.com

Bridlington Tel: 01262 673 474
25 Prince Street, Bridlington, East Yorkshire,YO15 2NP
E-mail/www: bridlington@ytbtic.co.uk
www.discoveryorkshirecoast.com

Danby Tel: 01439 772 737
The Moors Centre, Lodge Lane, Danby, Whitby, North
Yorkshire, YO21 2NB
E-mail/www: moorscentre@ytbtic.co.uk
www.moors.uk.net

PLACES OF INTEREST

Doncaster Tel: 01302 734 309
Central Library, Waterdale, Doncaster, South Yorkshire,
DN1 3JE
E-mail/www: tourist.information@doncaster.gov.uk

Easingwold Tel: 01347 821 530
Chapel Lane, Easingwold, York, YO61 3AE
E-mail/www: easingwold@ytbtic.co.uk
www.hambleton.gov.uk www.herriotcountry.com

Filey Tel: 01723 518 000
The Evron Centre, John Street, Filey, North Yorkshire,
YO14 9DW
E-mail/www: filey@ytbtic.co.uk
www.discoveryorkshirecoast.com www.e-sbc.co.uk

Grassington Tel: 01756 752 774
National Park Centre, Colvend, Hebden Road,
Grassington, North Yorkshire, BD23 5LB
E-mail/www: grassington@ytbtic.co.uk
www.yorkshiredales.org www.destinationdales.org

Great Ayton Tel: 01642 722 835
High Green Car Park, Great Ayton, Middlesbrough, TS9
6BJ
E-mail/www: greatayton@ytbtic.co.uk
www.hambleton.gov.uk www.herriotcountry.com

Halifax Tel: 01422 368 725
Piece Hall, Halifax, West Yorkshire, HX1 1RE
E-mail/www: halifax@ytbtic.co.uk

Harrogate Tel: 01423 537 300
Royal Baths Assembly Rooms, Crescent Road,
Harrogate, HG1 2RR
E-mail/www: tic@harrogate.gov.uk
www.harrogate.gov.uk/tourism

Hawes Tel: 01969 667 450
Dales Countryside Museum, Station Yard, Hawes, North
Yorkshire, DL8 3NT
E-mail/www: hawes@ytbtic.co.uk
www.yorkshiredales.org www.destinationdales.org

Haworth Tel: 01535 642 329/647 721
2-4 West Lane, Haworth, Keighley, West Yorkshire,
BD22 8EF
E-mail/www: haworth@ytbtic.co.uk
www.visithaworth.com

Hebden Bridge Tel: 01422 843 831
1 Bridge Gate, Hebden Bridge, West Yorkshire, HX7 8EX
E-mail/www: hebdenbridge@ytbtic.co.uk

Helmsley Tel: 01439 770 173
The Old Town Hall, Market Place, Helmsley, North Yorkshire, YO62 5BL
E-mail/www: helmsley@ytbtic.co.uk
www.ryedale.gov.uk/tourism

Holmfirth Tel: 01484 222 444
49-51 Huddersfield Road, Holmfirth, West Yorkshire, HD9 1JP
E-mail/www: holmfirth.tic@kirkleesmc.gov.uk

Hornsea Tel: 01964 536 404
120 Newbegin, Hornsea, HU18 1PB
E-mail/www: hornsea@ytbtic.co.uk
www.discoveryorkshirecoast.com

Horton-in-Ribblesdale Tel: 01729 860 333
Pen-y-ghent Café, Horton-in-Ribblesdale, Settle, North Yorkshire, BD24 0HE
E-mail/www: horton@ytbtic.co.uk
www.yorkshiredales.org www.destinationdales.org

Huddersfield Tel: 01484 223 200
3, Albion Street, Huddersfield, West Yorkshire, HD1 2NW
E-mail/www: huddersfield.tic@kirkleesmc.gov.uk

Hull - Paragon Street Tel: 01482 223 559
1 Paragon Street, Hull, HU1 3NA
E-mail/www: hullparagon@ytbtic.co.uk
www.hullcc.gov.uk/visithull

Humber Bridge Tel: 01482 640 852
North Bank Viewing Area, Ferriby Road, Hessle, HU13 0LN
E-mail/www: humberbridge@ytbtic.co.uk
www.eastriding.gov.uk

Ilkley Tel: 01943 602 319
Station Road, Ilkley, West Yorkshire, LS29 8HA
E-mail/www: ilkley@ytbtic.co.uk www.visitilkley.com

Ingleton Tel: 015242 41 049
Community Centre, Ingleton, Carnforth, North Yorkshire, LA6 3HG
E-mail/www: ingleton@ytbtic.co.uk
www.yorkshiredales.org www.destinationdales.org

Knaresborough Tel: 01423 866 886
9 Castle Courtyard, Market Place, Knaresborough,
North Yorkshire, HG5 8AE
E-mail/www: www.harrogate.gov.uk/tourism

Leeds Tel: 0113 242 5242
PO Box 244, Gateway Yorkshire, The Arcade, City
Station, Leeds, LS1 1PL
E-mail/www: tourinfo@leeds.gov.uk
www.leeds.gov.uk

Leeming Bar Tel: 01677 424 262
Great North Road, Leeming Bar, Bedale, North
Yorkshire, DL8 1DT
E-mail/www: leeming@ytbtic.co.uk www.ytb.org.uk

Leyburn Tel: 01969 623 069
4, Central Chambers, Market Place, Leyburn, North
Yorkshire, DL8 5BB
E-mail/www: leyburn@ytbtic.co.uk
www.yorkshiredales.org www.destinationdales.org

Malham Tel: 01729 830 363
Malham National Park Centre, Malham, Skipton, North
Yorkshire, BD23 4DA
E-mail/www: malham@ytbtic.co.uk
www.yorkshiredales.org www.destinationdales.org

Malton Tel: 01653 600 048
58 Market Place, Malton, North Yorkshire, YO17 7LW
E-mail/www: malton@ytbtic.co.uk
www.ryedale.gov.uk/tourism

Northallerton Tel: 01609 776 864
The Applegarth Car Park, Northallerton, North
Yorkshire, DL7 8LZ
E-mail/www: northallerton@ytbtic.co.uk
www.hambleton.gov.uk www.herriotcountry.com

Otley Tel: 0113 247 7707
The Library, Boroughgate, Otley, LS21 3AH
E-mail/www: otley@ytbtic.co.uk www.leeds.gov.uk

Pateley Bridge Tel: 01423 711 147
18 High Street, Pateley Bridge, North Yorkshire, HG3
5AW
E-mail/www: www.harrogate.gov.uk/tourism

Pickering Tel: 01751 473 791
The Ropery, Pickering, North Yorkshire, YO18 8DY
E-mail/www: pickering@ytbtic.co.uk
www.ryedale.gov.uk/tourism

PLACES OF INTEREST

Reeth Tel: 01748 884 059
Hudson House, The Green, Reeth, Richmond, North
Yorkshire, DL11 6TB
E-mail/www: reeth@ytbtic.co.uk
www.yorkshiredales.org www.destinationdales.org

Richmond Tel: 01748 850 252
Friary Gardens, Victoria Road, Richmond, North
Yorkshire, DL10 4AJ
E-mail/www: richmond@ytbtic.co.uk
www.yorkshiredales.org www.destinationdales.org

Ripon Tel: 01765 604 625
Minster Road, Ripon, North Yorkshire, HG4 1QT
E-mail/www: www.harrogate.gov.uk/tourism

Rotherham Tel: 01709 835 904
Central Library, Walker Place, Rotherham, South
Yorkshire, S65 1JH
E-mail/www: tic@rotherham.gov.uk

Scarborough Tel: 01723 373 333
Unit 3, Pavilion House, Valley Bridge Road,
Scarborough, North Yorkshire, YO11 1UZ
E-mail/www: scarboroughtic@scarborough.gov.uk
www.discoveryorkshirecoast.com www.e-sbc.co.uk

Sedbergh Tel: 015396 20 125
72, Main Street, Sedbergh, Cumbria, LA10 5AD
E-mail/www: sedbergh@yorkshiredales.org.uk
www.yorkshiredales.org www.destinationdales.org

Selby Tel: 01757 703263
Park Street, Selby, N. Yorks.
E-mail/www:

Settle Tel: 01729 825 192
Town Hall, Cheapside, Settle, North Yorkshire, BD24
9EJ
E-mail/www: settle@ytbtic.co.uk
www.yorkshiredales.org www.destinationdales.org

Sheffield Tel: 0114 221 1900
1, Tudor Square, Sheffield, S1 2LA
E-mail/www: visitor@sheffield.gov.uk

Skipton Tel: 01756 792 809
35 Coach Street, Skipton, North Yorkshire, BD23 1LQ
E-mail/www: skipton@ytbtic.co.uk
www.yorkshiredales.org www.destinationdales.org

PLACES OF INTEREST

Sutton Bank Tel: 01845 597 426
Sutton Bank Visitor Centre, Sutton Bank, Thirsk, North
Yorkshire, YO7 2EH
E-mail/www: suttonbank@ytbtic.co.uk
www.moors.uk.net

Thirsk Tel: 01845 522 755
49, Market Place, Thirsk, N. Yorks, YO7 1HA
E-mail/www: thirsk@ytbtic.co.uk
www.hambleton.gov.uk www.herriotcountry.com

Todmorden Tel: 01706 818 181
15, Burnley Road, Todmorden, Lancashire, OL14 7BU
E-mail/www: todmorden@ytbtic.co.uk

Wakefield Tel: 01924 305 000/305 001
Town Hall, Wood Street, Wakefield, West Yorkshire,
WF1 2HQ
E-mail/www: tic@wakefield.gov.uk
www.visitwakefield.org

Wetherby Tel: 01937 582 151
Wetherby Library & Tourist Information Centre, 17
Westgate, Wetherby, West Yorkshire, LS22 4LL
E-mail/www: wetherby@ytbtic.co.uk
www.leeds.gov.uk

Whitby Tel: 01947 602 674
Langbourne Road, Whitby, North Yorkshire, YO21 1YN
E-mail/www: whitbytic@scarborough.gov.uk
www.discoveryorkshirecoast.com www.e-sbc.co.uk

Withernsea Tel: 01964 615 683
131 Queen Street, Withernsea, East Yorks, HU19 2DJ
E-mail/www: withernsea@ytbtic.co.uk
www.yorkshiredales.org www.destinationdales.org

York Tel: 01904 621 756
Exhibition Square, York, YO1 2HB
E-mail/www: tic@york-tourism.co.uk
www.visityork.org

York - Railway Station Tel: 01904 621 756
Outer Concourse, Railway Station, Station Road, York,
YO1 7HB
E-mail/www: www.visityork.org

MARKET DAYS

Barnsley	Tuesday, Wednesday, Friday & Saturday
Bedale	Tuesday
Bentham	Wednesday
Beverley	Wednesday (small) & Saturday (large)
Bingley	Wednesday & Friday. Local Produce - last Saturday in month
Bradford	Monday - Saturday, $\frac{1}{2}$ day closing Wednesday
Bridlington	Wednesday, Saturday, Sunday & Bank Holidays
Brighouse	Wednesday & Saturday
Castleford	Monday, Thursday, Friday and Saturday
Dewsbury	Wednesday & Saturday
Doncaster	Tuesday, Friday & Saturday. Farmers' Market First Wednesday of Month
Driffield	Thursday & Saturday
Easingwold	Friday
Elland	Friday
Featherstone	Thursday
Filey	Friday (End February to Christmas)
Goldthorpe	Tuesday & Saturday
Halifax	Piece Hall - Friday & Saturday. Westgate Market - indoor - Monday to Saturday ($\frac{1}{2}$ day closing Thursday). Borough market - indoor 6 days a week.
Hawes	Tuesday
Hebden Bridge	Thursday
Helmsley	Friday
Hemsworth	Monday, Tuesday, Friday & Saturday
Holmfirth	Thursday (indoor). Farmers' Market Sunday every 4 weeks.
Hornsea	Indoor - Wednesday, Friday, Sunday & Bank Holiday
Hoyland	Tuesday & Saturday
Huddersfield	Monday & Thursday. Indoor Monday to Saturday.
Hull	Friday & Saturday. Indoor Monday to Saturday.
Ingleton	Friday
Keighley	Monday - Saturday (not Tuesday afternoon)
Kirkbymoorside	Wednesday
Knaresborough	Wednesday
Leeds	Monday - Saturday, $\frac{1}{2}$ day closing Wednesday

Leyburn	Friday. Farmers' Market - every 4th Saturday
Malton	Saturday
Masham	Wednesday & Saturday
Mexborough	Monday, Friday & Saturday
Normanton	Tuesday & Saturday
Northallerton	Wednesday & Saturday
Ossett	Tuesday & Friday
Otley	Tuesday (small), Friday & Saturday (main)
Penistone	Thursday
Pickering	Monday
Pocklington	Tuesday
Pontefract	Wednesday & Saturday. Indoor - Monday - Saturday ($^1/_2$ day closing Thursday)
Reeth	Friday
Richmond	Saturday. Indoor - Tuesday & Thursday. Farmers' Market - 3rd Saturday of each month
Ripon	Thursday
Rotherham	Monday, Friday & Saturday
Scarborough	Monday - Saturday
Sedbergh	Wednesday
Selby	Monday (main) & Saturday (small)
Settle	Tuesday
Sheffield	Castle Market - Monday to Saturday, $^1/_2$ day closing Thursday. Moor Market - Monday to Saturday.
Shipley	Friday & Saturday
Skipton	Monday, Wednesday, Friday and Saturday
South Elmsall	Tuesday, Friday & Saturday
Sowerby Bridge	Tuesday & Friday
Stokesley	Friday
Thirsk	Monday & Saturday
Todmorden	Wednesday, Friday & Saturday. Indoor - Monday, Wednesday, Thursday, Friday & Saturday.
Wakefield	Monday to Saturday (not Wednesdays). Indoor - Monday to Saturday ($^1/_2$ day Wednesday).
Wetherby	Thursday
Whitby	Tuesday, Saturday (am)
Withernsea	Sunday
Wombwell	Tuesday, Friday & Saturday
York	Newgate Market - Monday to Saturday

Aysgarth
Yorkshire Carriage Museum
Theme: Museum
Directions: Yore Mill, Church Bank, Aysgarth Falls.
Tel: 01969 663 399
Description: Collection of Victorian coaches housed in a mill overlooking Aysgarth Falls.

Barnard Castle
The Bowes Museum

Theme: Museum/Gallery
Directions: Signposted from the town
Tel: 01833 690 606
E-mail: info@bowesmuseum.org.uk
www: www.bowesmuseum.org.uk
Children: Welcome. Baby changing area available
Disabled: Most areas accessible. Audioguide available
Dogs: Guide dogs permitted in Museum. Dogs permitted in grounds.
Parking: Free Parking on site
Toilets: Toilets on site
Refreshments: Licensed Café
Shop: Gift shop
Open: Daily - 11am to 5pm
Closed Christmas Day, Boxing Day and New Year's Day
Charges: Adult: £6.00
Concession: £5.00
Under 16's: FREE
Description:
Founded by John Bowes and his French wife Josephine this magnificent museum, opened in 1892, houses one of Britain's finest collections of paintings, ceramics, furniture and textiles.

Set in 20 acres of parkland with a parterre garden the museum provides the perfect day out for all the family.

The museum has an active programme of temporary exhibitions, special events, musical concerts, outdoor theatre productions and family fun days, which run throughout the year.

Barnard Castle
The Otter Trust

Theme: Wildlife

Directions: Vale House Farm, near Bowes on the south side of the A66 Scotch Corner to Penrith road.

Tel: 01833 628 339

Parking: Parking on site

Toilets: Toilets on site

Refreshments: Available on site.

Shop: There is a gift shop on site

Open: April (or Good Friday if earlier) to October 10:30 am to 6:00 pm.

- Feeding Times: 12:00 Noon and 3:00pm.

Charges:

Adults: £5.00; **Senior Citizens**: £4.50; **Children** (3 - 15 years): £3.00

Coach Parties: **Adults**: £4.00; **Children** (3 - 15 years): £2.50

Organised School Parties: £1.50 per pupil - teachers free.

Description: The Otter Trust's North Pennines Reserve is the Trust's latest centre to be opened to the public. Here visitors can see British Otters in large semi-natural enclosures and a wealth of wildlife along the valley of the River Greta where hides have been installed overlooking pools frequented by waterfowl and waders.

The Otter Trust is famous for its release programme and to date over 100 otters bred by the Trust have been re-introduced into lowland England, to save the otter from extinction.

A branch of the famous Otter Trust. Visitors can roam over 230 acres of upland farmland, home in the spring to breeding Curlew, Oystercatcher, Lapwing, Snipe, Sandpiper, Redshank and Dipper. Black Grouse are regular visitors to this Reserve and Merlins are also seen here.

The River Greta flows in an enchanted valley right through the farm and the wildlife can be seen from strategically placed hides.

Rare breeds, including Exmoor ponies, White-faced Woodland sheep and Highland cattle, play their part in the conservation of this unspoilt countryside.

Refreshments and a Gift Shop will be found on site.

Barnsley (Cawthorne)
Cannon Hall Museum, Park & Gardens

Theme: House or House & Garden
Directions: 6 miles NW of Barnsley off the A635. leave MI at Junction 38, take the A637 to Barnsley and follow signs to Cannon Hall.
Address: Cannon Hall Museum, Park & Gardens Cawthorne, Barnsley, S75 4AT.
Tel: 01226 790270
Fax: 01226 792117
E-mail: cannonhall@barnsley.gov
www: barnsley.gov.uk
Facilities: Parking, toilets, refreshments, gifts & souvenirs available on site.
Open:
- **April - October:**
- Wednesday - Friday 10.30am - 5.00pm;
- Saturday and Sunday 12 noon - 5.00pm.
- (Last admission at 4.15pm.)
- **November, December and March:**
- Sun only: 12 noon - 4.00pm.
- **January and February: Closed.**

Description: Cannon Hall was the home of the Spencer-Stanhope family for over two hundred years and was remodelled by the architect John Carr from the 1760s. In 1957 it opened its doors as a museum. Step inside and you will find a treasure house of paintings, furniture, glassware and pottery and also Charge, the Regimental Museum of the 13th/18th Hussars (QMO). House trails available for children.

Set in 70 acres of historic parkland, with a Walled Garden and magnificent displays of rhododendrons, the site offers year-round events and an award- winning schools education programme. Refreshments are available at weekends in the Victorian Kitchen café.

Barnsley (Cawthorne)
Cannon Hall Open Farm

Theme: Farm, Farm Visitor Centre or Farm Shop
Directions: Follow signs from junction 38 of the MI.
Tel: 01226 790427
www: www.cannonhallfarm.co.uk
Description: Award winning attraction. Huge variety of animals. Home produced beef, pork & lamb.Barnsley

Barnsley
Elsecar Heritage Centre

Theme: Heritage Centre

Address: Wath Road, Elsecar, Barnsley, S74 8HJ
Tel: 01226 740 203
Description: An exciting Science and History Centre, offering an interesting and fun day out for all the family.

Barnsley
Elsecar Steam Railway

Theme: Rail Experience
Address: Wath Road, Elsecar, Barnsley, S74 8HJ
Tel: 01226 740203
Description: Between Rockingham Station at Elsecar to the Hemingfield Basin on the historic Dearne and Dove Canal. Picnic sites and amenities will be added to complete the Elsecar Steam Railway experience.

Barnsley
Old Moor Wetland Centre

Theme: Wildlife
Address: Manvers Way, Broomhill, Wombwell
Tel: 01226 751 593
Description: A 250 acre nature reserve with a variety of wetland habitats, in South Yorkshire's Dearne Valley.

Batley
Bagshaw Museum

Theme: Museum
Address: Wilton Park, Batley, WF17 0AS
Tel: 01924 326155
Description: Step straight from an Ancient Egyptian tomb into the tropical enchantment of the rainforest.

Batley
Batley Art Gallery

Theme: Arts Gallery or Centre
Address: Market Place, Batley, WF17 5DA
Tel: 01484 221964
Description: Continual programme of temporary exhibitions including art, craft, photography & sculpture.

Batley
Butterfly Conservation Centre

Theme: Conservation
Address: Wilton Park, Batley, WF17 0AS
Tel: 01924 326264
Description: A rich assortment of native butterflies many of which are close to disappearing in the wild.

Batley
Mill Discount Department Store

Theme: Shopping
Directions: M62 – J27, A62, A652
M62 – J28, A653, B6124
M1 – J40, A638, B6128
Address: Bradford Road, Batley, WF17 5LZ
Contact: Tourist Information Centre
Tel: 01924 426670
Fax: 01924 446096
E-mail: info@themillbatley.com
www: www. themillbatley.com
Children: Fully supervised crèche open till 4pm daily.
Disabled: Access to all areas. Toilets. Wheelchairs available, please pre-book to avoid disappointment.
Dogs: Guide dogs only allowed inside the buildings.
Parking: Free car and coach parking.
Toilets: Male, Female, Baby Changing Facilities.
Refreshments: Restaurant on the third floor.
Open: All year excluding Christmas Day. Monday to Saturday 9.30am to 5.30pm – Sundays and Bank Holidays 11.00am to 5.00pm.
Description: One of the largest Mill retail outlets in the UK attracting more than 1 million visitors a year. A totally new concept in discount shopping offering massive savings in a unique department format.
• The four floors together with an external parade sell heavily discounted products from designer fashion brands to everything for the stylish home. With over 40 retailers trading more than 300 brands over a total of 122,000 square feet, including Elle, Pilot, Lee Cooper, Suits You, Liz Claiborne, Puma, Leeds United, Event Jewellery, Scent to You, Ponden Mill and the Yorkshire phenomenon Readmans, (famous for selling top quality brands at bargain prices), it's an excellent shopping and leisure experience and a great day out for all the family, with events and entertainment during school holidays and designated weekends.
• The complex is situated at the heart of Brontë country and surrounded by places of interest for all the family.

Whatever your preferences, the on-site Tourist Information Centre will help you plan your next move, and even your next visit to the area.

The Mill Discount Department Store, Batley
A Great Day Out For All the Family

Batley
Oakwell Hall Country Park

Theme: Museum
Address: Nutter Lane, Birstall, Nr. Batley, WF17 9LG
Tel: 01924 326240
Description: This beautiful Elizabethan manor house, built in 1583, has delighted visitors for centuries.

Batley
Red Brick Mill

Theme: Shopping
Directions: Bradford Road, Batley.
Tel: 01924 460044
Description: Beautifully converted Victorian weaving mill, now home to a variety of shops. Establishing itself as a centre for arts, crafts and culture.

Batley
Skopos Motor Museum

Theme: Museum
Directions: Alexandra Mills, Alexandra Road, Batley
Tel: 01924 444 423
Description: Holds some of the most magnificent and diverse pieces of motoring genius ever assembled. Watch experts go about meticulous restoration work.

Bedale
Bedale Museum

Theme: Museum
Address: Bedale Hall, Bedale, N. Yorks, DL8 1AA
Contact:
Tel: 01677 423 797 **Fax:** 01677 425 393
Description: A fascinating little museum depicting the life of ordinary people. The centrepiece is the Bedale hand drawn fire engine dating from 1748.

Bedale
Big Sheep and Little Cow Farm

Theme: Farm, Farm Visitor Centre or Farm Shop
Address: Big Sheep & Little Cow Farm, Aiskew, Bedale, N Yorks, DL8 1AW
Tel: 01677 422 125
Description: Visit a fun, friendly, hands-on farm. Lambs, piglets, cattle sheep and pigs. Pony rides.

Bedale (Crakehall)
Crakehall Water Mill
Theme: Mill or Windmill

Directions: On main road out of Crakehall
Address: Little Crakehall, Bedale, N. Yorks, DL8 1HU
Tel: 01677 423 240
Facilities: Parking, toilets and refreshments on site.
Open:
- Easter to 30th September
- Wednesday to Sunday 10.00 am to late evening and Bank Holidays.

Charges:
- Adults/Students: £2.00

Description: A working water corn mill on the site of a mill mentioned in the Domesday Book. The mill still produces stoneground flour, which is available at the mill and in local shops. Tea room/café, Holiday lets, B&B.

Bedale (Thorp Perrow)
Thorp Perrow Arboretum & The Falcons of Thorp Perrow
Theme: Arboretum (and Falconry Centre)
Directions: 4 miles from Leeming Bar on the A1, via Bedale, the B6268, and the minor road towards Well.
Address: The Administrator, Thorp Perrow Arboretum, Bedale, N. Yorks, DL8 2PR
Tel: 01677 425 323
E-mail: louise@thorpperrow.freeserve.co.uk
www: www.thorpperrow.com
Disabled: Accessible to wheelchairs, and facilities for the disabled are available at the tearoom. An electric wheelchair is available free of charge but must be booked prior to visit. Tel: 01677 427 203.
Dogs: Welcome but MUST be kept on a lead at all times.

Facilities: Parking, toilets, refreshments & shop on site.
Open: Arboretum open daily from dawn to dusk. The bird centre and tearoom will be open from the 15th of February to mid November. Thereafter at weekends only from 11.00 am - 3.00 pm. Flying times 11.30 am, 1.30pm and 3.30pm March to 26th October. *(Thereafter 11.30am & 1.30pm)*
Charges: To Arboretum and Falcons of Thorp Perrow
- Adults: £5.25 • OAPs and students: £4.00 • Child (Under 4 free): £2.75 • Family (2+2): £15.00 • Family (2+4): £19.00

Events: Many events throughout the season.
Description: The Arboretum has 85 acres of woodland walks and is one of the largest and rarest collections of trees and shrubs in England. It holds four National Collections – Ash, Lime, Walnut and Laburnam, and also embraces a 19c pinetum and a medieval spring wood. Thorp Perrow has something to offer all year round. Thousands of naturalised daffodils in the spring, followed with blossom, carpets of bluebells and bold drifts of wild flowers. Later in  the year the autumn foliage provides dramatic effects and stunning colours.

The Falcons of Thorp Perrow is a captive breeding and conservation centre that gives visitors the opportunity to learn about birds of prey, with the enjoyment of hands on experience for all the family.

Beverley

Description: A medieval town surrounded on three sides by ancient common lands, known as Beverley Pastures. • The Minster was founded early in the 8th century, although damage caused during the Viking invasions and the Norman Conquest means that the present building only dates back to 1220. Today, it's one of the finest examples of a Gothic church of cathedral size in Europe. • Also founded in this era is St. Mary's Church, which was initially a chapel of ease for the town's residents. Inside the church is a carving of the 'Jolly rabbit', which is said to have been the inspiration for the white rabbit in Lewis Carol's 'Alice in Wonderland'. • Like York, Beverley saw the building of Medieval Bars to protect the town. North Bar is the sole survivor of four or possibly five gateways constructed in the 15th century. • With shops famed for its merchandise and fine Medieval and Georgian architecture, Beverley is perhaps one of the most beautiful towns in Britain.

Beverley
Beverley Minster

Theme: Cathedral or Cathedral Ruins
Description: The present church, the third building on the site is intimately associated with Saint John of Beverley, whose remains lie in the nave. Beverley became a place of sanctuary and pilgrimage in the middle ages. Henry V came to the Minster to give thanks after the battle of Agincourt. Building of the present church commenced c. 1220.

Beverley
Beverley Races

Theme: Horse Racing
Address: York Road, Beverley, East Yorks, HU17 8QZ
Tel: 01482 882645
Description: The only racecourse serving East Yorkshire.

Beverley
Museum of Army Transport

Theme: Museum
Directions: Close to Beverley Minister it has a large car park and is signposted 'Military Museum'.
Tel: 01482 860 445
www:
www.army.mod.uk/ceremonialandheritage/museums/details/m021tran.htm
Description: Unique collection of Road, Rail, Sea and Air exhibits from horse drawn and Armoured Fighting vehicles, to Staff cars and motorcycles, representing over 100 years of Army Transport. Of particular interest are the Rolls used by Field Marshal Montgomery in North West Europe and the wagon used by Lord Roberts in the Boer War

Beverley
Skidby Mill

Theme: Mill or Windmill
Directions: Just off the A614 near the village of Skidby and surrounded by picturesque countryside.
Description: There has been a windmill in Skidby since 1388. This mill, Built in 1821, has been grinding grain for nearly two centuries! • Also home to the Museum of East Riding Rural Life.

Bolton Abbey
Bolton Abbey and Estate

Theme: Scenic View or Walk and Family day out
Directions: B6160 off A59 between Skipton and Harrogate.
Tel: 01756 718 009
E-mail: tourism@boltonabbey.com
www: www.boltonabbey.com
Disabled: Electric wheelchairs are available; they give access to the Priory Ruins, riverside, Cavendish Pavillion, Strid Wood and the Strid.
Dogs: Dogs are welcome, but they are not allowed on the moorland access areas.
Parking: The Estate has three car parks with information points – tickets are valid for all three car parks on the day of issue.
Toilets: Toilet facilities are available in all three car parks, all have disabled and nappy changing facilities.
Refreshments: The Estate hosts picnic sites, caféterias, licensed restaurants and hotels.
Shop: Three gift shops carry an extensive range of quality giftware.
Open: Open every day except Christmas Day.
Charges: Vehicles £4.00. Disabled badge holder £2.00. Occupants free.
Description: The Yorkshire estate of the Duke and Duchess of Devonshire.

- Explore this historic estate with its medieval buildings and woodland walks, or simply relax and enjoy a picnic whilst the children play.
- As the name suggests Bolton Abbey was originally a large monastic estate, based around the 12th century priory. Legend has it that the Priory was established in 1120 by Cecily de Romille as an expression of her grief following the drowning of her son in the near by Strid.

The Estate has over 80 miles of footpaths through some of the most spectacular scenery in England. There are walks alongside the river Wharfe, with its peaceful shallows and fearsome Strid, through Strid Wood, with its rich variety of wildlife, and as a complete contrast some that cross the exposed purple heights of heather moorland.

Bradford

Description: There's a lot to see and do in Bradford City Centre, whatever the time of year. If your passion is history and heritage, take your pick from a series of **FREE City Centre Trails** which offer a revealing insight into Bradford's rich past—from its stunning buildings to impressive public art. Right in the heart of the city you will find the magnificent civic building City Hall, home to the **Tourist Information Centre**, overlooking Centenary Square; the public square is used as a prestigious venue for outdoor events and entertainment.

One of the city's highlights is a visit to the **National Museum of Photography, Film & Television** (p31) with its five floors of interactive displays and three popular cinemas including eye-popping 3D IMAX. Each year, the museum hosts three national film festivals.

Images of a different kind are on view at **The Colour Museum** (p30) where the magic of Colour is brought to life. This unique museum is dedicated to the history, development and technology of Colour.

Bradford Cathedral (p29), a beautiful building set in tranquil gardens, dates back to the 15th century. It is full of interest relating to Bradford heritage and has William Morris stained glass windows.

The **Leisure Exchange** at Vicar Lane which opened in December 2001, hosts a Hollywood Bowl and sixteen-screen Cine World cinema showing everything from block-busters to Bollywood films.

There are plenty of attractions for shoppers with a host of high street stores and independent shops combining to offer choice and quality. The main shopping areas include Broadway, Darley Street, North Parade and Kirkgate plus the new-look Kirkgate Shopping Centre. The Grade I listed Wool Exchange is not to be missed! The former hub of the city's famous wool trade has been converted into a quality retail Centre including a large Waterstone's bookstore and Starbucks Coffee Shop.

Multi-million pound developments are transforming the city centre into a great place to live, work and enjoy. These include a completely refurbished Sunwin House department store, a new-look Ostler Centre and stylish new city apartments in Little Germany and overlooking Centenary Square.

PLACES OF INTEREST

For a lively night out anytime, join the crowds heading for Bradford's West End with its lively mix of late bars and places to eat.

For more on things to see and do in Bradford City Centre, or for copies of the **FREE City Centre Trails**, or the District Visitor Guide, contact **Bradford Tourist Information Centre** on: 01274 433678, or email **tourist.information@bradford.gov.uk**

Over eight million visitors a year, come from far and wide to the Bradford District. Many head for **Haworth** (p49), the literary village associated with the Brontë sisters or the rugged moors around **Ilkley** (p58).

Others come to see the Victorian model industrial village of **Saltaire**—a UNESCO World Heritage Site, and the **Salts Mill** (p32) complex, which houses the world's largest collection by Bradford-born artist David Hockney. The Tourist Information Centres can provide you with information on places to visit, accommodation bookings and travel details.

There are Tourist Information Centres at

City Hall, Centenary Square, **Bradford**, BD1 1HY
  Telephone 01274 433 678 Fax 01274 739 067
www.visitbradford.com

2-4, West Lane, **Haworth**, BD22 8EF
  Telephone 01535 642 329 Fax 01274 647 721
www.visithaworth.com

Station Road, **Ilkley**, LS29 8HA
  Telephone 01943 602 319 Fax 01943 603 795
www.visitilkley.com

All have the following opening hours:
24th March – 18th October 2003: 0930 – 1730hrs
20th October – 1st March 2004: 0930 – 1700hrs

Bradford and Ilkley TICs' closed Sundays

Bradford
Alhambra Theatre
Theme: Theatre or Playhouse
Address: Morley Street, Bradford, BD7 1AJ
Tel: 01274 432375
www: www.bradford-theatres.co.uk
Description: Built in 1914 and refurbished in 1986 with stunning results, it is a testimony to the splendour of the Edwardian music hall era.

Bradford
Alhambra Theatre Studio

Theme: Theatre or Playhouse
Address: The Studio, Bradford, BD1
Tel: 01274 432375
www: www.bradford-theatres.co.uk
Description: Located in the heart of the city centre and adjacent the Alhambra Theatre. Provides the perfect setting for theatrical events (both theatre and cabaret style). Full disabled access to the auditorium with male and female adapted foyer toilet facilities.

Bradford
Apollo Canal Cruises

Theme: Boat Hire or Cruise
Directions: Shipley 4 miles from Bradford.
Tel: 01274 595914
Description: A Waterbus service operates from Saltaire to Hirst Wood and Shipley, including a trip through a lock. ● Cruise along the Leeds-Liverpool canal through stunning countryside and historic villages.

Bradford
Bolling Hall

Theme: Museum
Address: Bowling Hall Road, Bradford, BD4 7LP
Tel: 01274 723057
www: www.bradford.gov.uk/tourism/museums/
Description: A largely 17th century manor house incorporating a tudor pele tower, with a wing altered in the late 18th century. • Best known for its splendid array of 17th century oak North Country Furniture and for its huge window full of stained glass Coats of Arms.

Bradford
Bracken Hall Countryside Centre

Theme: Museum
Address: Glen Road, Baildon, Bradford, BD17 5EA
Tel: 01274 584140
Description: Displays and temporary exhibitions relating to the local landscape, archaeology, history, geology and natural history of the area. Many of the displays are interactive, and a programme of regular children's activities and family walks take place.

Bradford
Bradford Cathedral

Theme: Cathedral or Cathedral Ruins
Address: Bradford Cathedral, 1 Stott Hill, Bradford, BD1 4EH
Tel: 01274 777720
Fax: 01274 777730
www: www.bradford.gov.uk/tourism/trails/cathedral
Disabled: Most of the Cathedral is accessible. Ramps available soon. Induction Loop facility. Adapted toilet. One disabled parking space in grounds.
Dogs: Only guide dogs.
Parking: Pay & Display car parks in the City Centre.
Toilets: Available.
Refreshments: Can be booked by groups.
Shop: Cards and souvenirs.
Facilities: Beautiful gardens.
Open:
- Monday - Saturday 08.30 - 16.30.
- Sunday for services at 08.00, 10.00 and 18.30

Charges: Admission Free. Educational visits for groups - fee according to programme.
Description: Bradford's most ancient place of worship, friendly, peaceful, and fascinating. Beautiful building set in city centre gardens.

Many special features including William Morris windows, embroidery designed by Ernest Sichel, and much Bradford heritage.

Bradford
Brontë Birthplace

Theme: Historic Place
Directions: Bus 607 or 697 from Bradford. By road, just off the B6145.
Address: Brontë Birthplace, 72/74 Market Street, Thornton, Bradford, BD13 3HF
Contact: Barbara Whitehead.
Tel: 01274 830 849
www: brontebirthplace.org.uk
Children: Welcome.
Disabled: Not suitable for wheelchairs.
Dogs: Yes.
Parking: In nearby street.
Toilets: Yes, one.
Refreshments: By prior arrangement.

Shop: Small display
Open: 1ˢᵗ April - 30ᵗʰ September ● 12.00 noon - 16.00
Sundays and Tuesdays only ● Other times by
appointment.
Charges: Adults: £3.00 ● Students/OAP's: £2.50 ●
Children (5 – 16): £1.50 ● Children (under 5): Free.
Description: The former parsonage where Charlotte,

Branwell, Emily and Anne
Brontë were born. This
comfortable family home
is being restored to its
Brontë period. It is a
starrred Grade II listed
building.

Bradford
Colour Museum, The

Theme: Museum
Directions: In the centre of Bradford, just off the
B6144, a short distance from the city's Metro
Interchange and Forster Square.
Address: Perkin House, Providence Street, Bradford,
West Yorkshire, BD1 2PW
Tel: 01274 390 955
Fax: 01274 392 888
E-mail: museum@sdc.org.uk
www: www.sdc.org.uk
Disabled: Lift and toilet facilities available in the
museum. Several steps leading to the workshop room
can make access difficult for wheelchair users.
Dogs: Only Registered Assistance Dogs allowed.
Toilets: On site, including disabled and nappy changing
facilities.
Shop: Selling souvenirs and educational toys & books.
Open: Tuesday to Saturday 10:00am to 4:00pm. Last
admission 3:30pm.
Charges: Adult: £2.00 • Concession £1.50 • Family
ticket: £4.00
Description:
We guarantee that you've never seen anything like it!

Why?

Because the Colour Museum is unique.

Dedicated to the history, development and technology of
colour, it's the *Only* museum of its kind in Europe. A
truly colourful experience for both kids and adults, it's
fun, it's informative and it's well worth a visit.

Bradford
National Museum of Photography, Film & Television

Theme: Museum
Directions: 2 miles from the end of the M606 in City Centre.
Address: NMPFT, Bradford, W. Yorks, BD1 1NQ
Tel: 01274 202 030 **Fax:** 01274 394 540
E-mail: talk.nmpft@nmsi.ac.uk
www: www.nmpft.org.uk
Children: Baby changing facilities available.
Disabled: Fully accessible.
Dogs: Guide dogs only.
Parking: Special rates available at the Hall Ings NCP on production of a voucher from the Museum Box Office.
Toilets: Toilets on site
Refreshments: Intermission Café-Restaurant serves snacks and meals.
Shop: Yes
Open: 10am to 6pm; Tuesday to Sunday & Bank/Main School Holiday Mondays.
Charges: Museum admission is FREE, charges apply for the cinemas and some exhibitions.
Description: Explore the ten free interactive galleries where you can ride a magic carpet, read the news or look back at your TV favourites from yesteryear. Don't forget to take in an IMAX film on a screen so huge you actually become part of the action. Insight: Collections and Research Centre, opens up the treasures of the Museum's Collection like never before. Exhibitions, tours and talks allow visitors to discover some of the Museum's wonderful artefacts. There's something for everyone at the NMPFT, it's a great day out.

Bradford
Peace Museum

Theme: Museum
Directions: 10 Piece Hall Yard (Opp Waterstones).
Tel: 01274 434 009
www: www.bradford.gov.uk
Description: Unique in the U.K., covering peace history, non-violence and conflict resolution.

Bradford
Saltaire United Reformed Church

Theme: Church or Church Ruins
Directions: Beside the canal in Saltaire.
Address: Victoria Road, Saltaire, Shipley BD18 3LA
Contact: Len Morris
Tel: 01274 597 894

E-mail: len.morris@physics.org
www: www.saltaireurc.info
Disabled: Disabled facilities – none.
Parking: In Church grounds – FREE for visitors.
Toilets: Available when café is open.
Open:
- Easter to September daily 14:00 to 16:00
- October to Easter Sundays only 14:00 - 16:00
- Services every Sunday 10:30 -11:30

Charges: Admission is FREE but a voluntary donation is welcome.
Awards: Part of a World Heritage Site.
Description: Built in the Classical style it was the first public building in the village of Saltaire, opened in 1859. The entrance is up six steps under a portico supported by six unfluted Corinthian columns, topped by a fretted tower. Fittingly, the Mausoleum built onto the church contains the remains of Sir Titus Salt himself: Inside are hollow Corinthian columns with beautiful Scagliola exteriors, fashioned by Italian craftsmen. Two ornate chandeliers ormolu and cut glass hang from the ceiling. Refreshments are available on Sunday afternoons.

Bradford
Salts Mill

Theme: Museum
Address: Victoria Road, Saltaire, Bradford, BD18 3LB
Tel: 01274 531163
Description: 3 floors which have been converted into a world of art, music, books, flowers and shops. Houses the world's largest collection by artist David Hockney.

Bradford
Shipley Glen Cable Tramway

Theme: Scenic View, Walk or Ride
Address: Prod Lane, Baildon, Shipley, BD17 5BN
Tel: 01274 589010/492026
Description: A narrow gauge cable hauled tramway
built in 1895 to serve the delights of Shipley Glen.

Bradford
St. George's Concert Hall

Theme: Concert or Music Hall
Address: Bridge Street, Bradford, BD1 1JS
Tel: 01274 432375
www: www.bradford-theatres.co.uk
Description: Bringing the cream of touring music,
comedy and variety shows to the region.

Bradford
St. Leonards Farm Park

Theme: Farm, Farm Visitor Centre or Farm Shop
Address: Chapel Lane, off Station Road, Esholt,
Shipley, West Yorkshire, BD17 7RB
Tel: 01274 598795
www: www.stleonardsfarm.com
Description: Award-winning farm in Esholt Village.
(Original home of T.V.'s Emmerdale). Lots of different
animals, some of which you can feed.

Brandsby (York)
Acorn Industries

Theme: Craft Workshop or Shop
Directions: Brandsby, 15 miles North of York on B1363
Tel: 01347 888 217
Description: High class furniture using solid timbers
including oak, mahogany, walnut, elm and chestnut.

Bridlington
Bayle Museum

Theme: Museum
Tel: 01262 674 308
E-mail: charity@themail.co.uk
www: www.bayle.bridlington.net
Open: May to September, Monday to Friday
10am to 4pm • Last admission 3.30pm.
Charges: Adults: £1 • Children: 50p • OAPs: £1
Description: Housed in 12th century Augustinian
gateway. Victorian kitchens, items of military and
agricultural interest and reconstructed prison cell.

Bridlington
Flamborough Head

Theme: Land or Seascape
Description: Where locals gathered in 1779 when John Paul Jones, a Scotsman who became the "father" of the US navy battled with HMS Serapis during the American War of Independence. When asked to surrender, because his own ship was sinking, Jones shouted "I have not yet begun to fight" and captured the British frigate.

Bridlington
Old Penny Memories

Theme: Museum
Directions: Next to the Hook and Parrot public house.
Tel: 01262 608400 01262 603341
www: www.oldpennymemories.co.uk
Description: Explore the world of the penny arcade and the history of coin – operated amusement games.

Bridlington
World of Rock

Theme: Factory Tour and Shop
Directions: 2 miles outside Bridlington
Tel: 01262 678 525
Description: Learn the secret of rock, fudge, toffee and chocolate making unfold before your very eyes.

Brighouse
Smith Art Gallery

Theme: Arts Gallery or Centre
Address: Halifax Road, Brighouse, HD6 2AF
Tel: 01484 719222
Description: A purpose built late Victorian Art Gallery. A permanent collection of Victorian paintings and a programme of temporary exhibitions.

Castleford
Freeport Castleford Retail and Leisure Village

Theme: Shopping
Directions: From M62/J32, Castleford/ Glasshoughton
Tel: 01977 520153
www: www.freeportplc.com
Description: Big name fashion brands to kitchenware & china at up to 50% off high street prices.

Clapham
Ingleborough

Theme: Land or Seascape

Description: At 2,373 ft, Ingleborough, with its famous flat topped profile, is perhaps best known of the Yorkshire Dales' famous "Three Peaks". (see also Pen-y-ghent (p109) and Whernside (p61)). ● The distinctive shape is due to a broad cap of millstone grit atop a broader plateau of carboniferous limestone. Streams running off the millstone grit meet limestone rock further down the slopes where they disappear underground into potholes and caverns. ● The surface limestone offers one of the best examples of upland limestone pavements in the UK. ● On a clear day you can see the Irish Sea, the Isle of Man and the Lake District.

Clapham
Ingleborough Show Cave

Theme: Cave or Caves

Directions: Clapham village is off the A65 Leeds - Skipton - Kendal road on the Western edge of the Yorkshire Dales National Park.

Address: Ingleborough Cave, Clapham, LA2 8EE

Tel: 015242 51242

E-mail: info@ingleboroughcave.co.uk

www: www.ingleboroughcave.co.uk

Children: Accessible by pushchair.

Dogs: Allowed on lead.

Parking: In Clapham Village.

Toilets: Yes (regret not disabled).

Refreshments: Light refreshments at the Cave.

Shop: Yes

Open: Daily 10am. – 5pm. (4pm. Winter months). Midweek visits during winter months by prior arrangement only.

Charges:- Adults:- £4.50; **Children:-** 2.50; **Family (2 Adults + 2 Children):-** £12

Events: Father Christmas Grotto weekends in December.

Description: Ingleborough Cave, a show cave since its discovery in 1837. Almost an hour long underground tour of 1km along the large and impressive outlet passages of the world famous Gaping Gill system with many formations and features, all spectacularly floodlit. Park in Clapham village and follow the river up the dale passing the lake and the woods of the Nature Trail to the cave (1½ miles). The cave is rarely affected by flooding, is accessible by pushchair and dogs are allowed on lead.

Coxwold (York)
Newburgh Priory

Theme: Priory or Priory Ruins
Address: Newburgh Priory, Coxwold, York, YO61 4AS
Tel: 01347 868 435
Open: 1st April to 30th June:
Sunday & Wednesday: House: 2.00 pm to 6.00 pm;
Grounds: 2.30pm - 4.45pm
Open Easter Sunday & Monday 2003
Charges: House & Grounds:
Adults: £5.00; Children £1.50
Grounds only:
Adults £2.50; Children FREE
Description: Home of the Earls of Fauconberg and
Wombwell family. Originally built in 1145 with Tudor,
Jacobean and Georgian additions. Family pictures and
furntiture as well as the tomb of Oliver Cromwell.

Coxwold (York)
Shandy Hall

Theme: Historic Building
Address: Shandy Hall, Coxwold, York, YO61 4AD
Tel: 01347 868 465
Fax: 01347 868 465
Description: Medieval building, little changed since
18th century. Large collection of Sterne's work. Prints,
medieval wall painting, walled garden.

Danby (Whitby)
Moors Centre TIC

Theme: Information Centre
Directions: In the north of the Park, 3/4 of a mile outside
Danby in the Esk Valley (OS Grid Ref: NZ 717 084)
Tel: 01439 772737
www: www.moors.uk.net
Description: At the very heart of the National Park
amidst the idyllic setting of the Esk Valley.

Doncaster
Earth Centre

Theme: Exhibition or Education Centre
Address: Denaby Main, Doncaster, DN12 4GA
Tel: 01709 513 933
www: www.earthcentre.org.uk
Description: Unique interactive exhibitions, fantastic
play areas, unusual gardens and 375 acre Country Park

Doncaster (Womersley)
Womersley Crafts & Herbs

Theme: Craft Shop
Address: Womersley, Doncaster, Yorkshire, DN6 9BH
Tel: 01977 620 294
Fax: 01977 620 200
E-mail: womersleycrafts@hotmail.com
www: www.womersleycrafts.co.uk
Open: All year
Charges: Admission: FREE
Awards: BBC Good Food Show 2002 **winner** of the **"Food Lovers' Fair Gold Award"**. Featured on The Kevin Woodford Series and Yorkshire TV's Tonight programme. Also a top 20 award winner in Henrietta Green's **"Food Lover's Guide to Great Britain"**.
Description: Founded in 1978 Womersley Crafts specialise in growing herbs and fruit which they use in their now famous Womersley Hall culinary condiments. These are offered all over the country to chefs, hotels, restaurants, delicatessens and the more discerning members of the public. • These full-bodied true-flavoured fruit vinegars have far wider uses than many people imagine. They can transform a salad dressing or vinaigrette, or can enrich and enliven sauces, both with starters or main courses, whether meat, poultry, fish or even pastas. They are delicious in stir fries and vegetables, they can be served hot or cold with fruit, puddings, pancakes, ice-cream etc. Their versatility, especially in the hands of an inventive chef, is quite amazing. • Womersley Herb Jellies are a familiar sight in kitchens and restaurants throughout the country. The distinctive colour and natural flavour are the hallmarks of their quality and because no gelatine is used, they are particularly useful to vegetarians. Not only do they make an ideal accompaniment to food, but because they are clear, entirely natural and 'loosely set', they may also be reduced to flavour sauces or added to roasts as an appetising and colourful glaze. You may also wish to try them with salads and sandwiches and in your own special recipes.
Product Range: • Fruit Vinegars • Fruit/Herb Blended Dressings • Herb Vinegars • Herb Jellies •Chutneys •Herb Plants • Dried Herbs & Spices • Herb Pillows & Wheat Bags • Aromatherapy Products • Essential Oils & Massage Oils • Toiletries, Perfumes and Room Sprays - including Gentlemen's Range • Candles • Painted Glassware • Pottery • Jewellery • Wood Turning •

Driffield (Foston-on-the-Wolds)
Cruckley Animal Farm

Theme: Farm, Farm Visitor Centre or Farm Shop

Address: Foston-on-the-Wolds, Driffeld, East Yorks, Y025 8BS

Contact: Sue and John Johnston

Tel: 01262 488337

E-mail: cruckley@aol.com

www: www.cruckley.co.uk

Children: Baby changing facilities. Play area.

Disabled: Fully disabled toilets.

Dogs: Our sheep request that you leave your dog in our shady, FREE car park.

Parking: FREE car and coach park.

Toilets: Including disabled, close to our FREE car park.

Refreshments: Tea room open daily from 11am.

Facilities: Tea Room and Shop. Hot & cold drinks, ices, sweets, home made cakes, gifts, etc.

Open: Daily 18th April to 30th September 2003 from 10.30 am to 5.30 pm.

Charges: Adults £3.25 ● OAPs £2.50 ● Children £2.00 ● ● Children 2 and under FREE

Awards: RBST approved conservation centre.

Description: A real working farm and Approved, Rare Breeds Centre ● Daily milking demonstration at 10.45 am approx. ● Large variety of farm animals ● Baby animals born throughout the season ● Safe 1½ mile walkway • Waterfowl lake, with nature reserve ● Tea room and gift shop ● Special rates for groups ● Educational tours for schools • Indoor & outdoor picnic areas ● Play area.

Driffield (Sledmere)
Sledmere House

Theme: House or House & Garden

Directions: Between Driffield and Malton on the B1251.

Tel: 01377 236 637

Description: Fine collection of antique furniture, pottery, paintings and rare books. Roman Catholic Chapel attached to the house has a most beautiful ceiling. Beautiful gardens and parkland.

Grassington

www: www.grassington.co.uk
Parking: At the National Park Centre car park.
Limited parking in the square
Toilets: At the National Park Centre car park.
Refreshments: Plenty of places in the village.
Description: The largest and one of the most popular villages in Upper Wharfedale, yet it retains much of its own character. The busy cobbled square and Main Street reflect a traditional working centre..

Grassington Festival is a must for two weeks each Summer. One of the really successful arts festivals with a programme every year mixing everything from poetry and comedy to string quartets.

The 23rd Grassington Festival is from the 13th to the 28th of June, 2003. **www.grassington-festival.org.uk**

The three Dickensian weekends in December each year are hugely popular. Complete with street vendors and entertainers in costume. Children and adults alike will love it.

The surrounding countryside is superb and abounds in networks of footpaths suitable for both the inexperienced and the more seasoned walker. Grass Wood, the last remains of the original forest, is now cared for by the Yorkshire Wildlife Trust and contains rare species of both flora and fauna.

Grassington Moor, at Yarnbury, was once a busy centre for lead mining. The old workings have been identified with plaques to help visitors recapture some of the dale's industrial past.

In the valley bottom, the Wharfe, renowned for its trout fishing, is also home to a variety of wildlife, including the colourful kingfisher and the large grey heron.

Grassington
Dales Kitchen

Theme: Refreshments (Licensed Tearooms & Brasserie)
Directions: Conveniently located at 51 Main Street.
Tel: 01756 753 208
Refreshments: Morning Coffee • Lunches • Savouries • Cream Teas
Awards: In the Egon Ronay Guide for 1994, 1995, 1996 & 1997

Grassington
Gemini Studios

Theme: Craft Workshop or Shop
Address: 51A, Main Street, Grassington, BD23 5AU
Tel: 01756 752 605
Description: Original Dales landscape art on display in 17th century barn. Jewellery design, commissions etc.

Grassington
Kilnsey Crag

Theme: Scenic View or Walk
Directions: 4 miles N of Grassington on the B6160.
Description: Imposing natural sight. The overhanging face of Kilnsey Crag is a popular challenge for climbers.

Grassington
Kilnsey Park, Trout Farm, Farm Shop & Children's Fishery

Theme: Leisure Park, Shopping, Farm Shop & Craft Shop
Speciality: Fish, Fishing and Food
Directions: Kilnsey is 4 miles N of Grassington on the B6160 road.
Tel: 01756 752 150
www: www.kilnseypark.co.uk
Refreshments: Restaurant to seat 50.
Shop: Deli, stocking local food, fresh fish products and gifts.
Facilities: Children and disabled visitors are all welcome. Dogs must be kept on a lead in the Park. Car parking and toilet facilities are available on site.
Open: All year from 9:00am to 5:30pm (dusk in winter)
Charges: £1 per head to the Craft Shop.
Description: Kilnsey Park is situated in the heart of the Yorkshire Dales.

- The fresh spring water helps produce delicious trout and provides water for adult and children's fishing. It is now put to a further new use generating electricity for the Shop and Restaurant.
- Other facilities include a conservation centre with red squirrels, a nature trail, trout feeding and viewing areas, children's playground and fly fishing ponds, a herb and alpine centre and a new rural craft shop.

The Restaurant produces home-made food sourced locally and the Estate Shop and Deli are stocked with Dales produce, including many fish dishes, venison and game from the estate.

Grassington
Kilnsey Trekking & Riding Centre

Theme: Recreation
Directions: Kilnsey is 4 miles N of Grassington on the B6160 road.
Tel: 01756 752 861 or 01756 753 369
Fax: 01756 752 957
E-mail: info@kilnseyriding.com
www: kilnseyriding.com
Disabled: Experienced staff and trustworthy ponies ensure disabled riders have a memorable day out.
Facilities: Children are very welcome. Parking, toilets and a snack machine are all available on site.
Open: Open all year weather permitting.
Description: Just a short walk from Kilnsey Park.

- A stable of safe and friendly ponies, suitable for experienced and novice riders alike. An ideal centre for exploring, on horseback, some of the finest scenery in England.
- Full days, half days, hours and a short river ride for small children and beginners.
- Group or individual lessons available.
- For the more experienced and adventurous rider follow the old green lanes which traverse the dramatic moorland scenery. Riders stay at traditional taverns and youth hostels. Rides can be varied to suit individuals and small groups.
- Prices on application.

Grassington (Appletreewick)
Parcevall Hall Gardens

Theme: Garden(s)
Directions: Skyreholme, near Appletreewick, off the B6160 or the B6265.
Tel: 01756 720 311
Description: Sixteen acres of beautiful woodland gardens set in magnificent Dales Countryside.

Grassington
Stump Cross Caverns

Theme: Showcave, Tea Room and Shop
Directions: Lies 5 miles East of Grassington on the B6265 road to Pateley Bridge.
Tel: 01756 752 780
www: www.stumpcrosscaverns.co.uk
Parking: Parking on site
Toilets: Toilets on site
Refreshments: Refreshments on site
Shop: Gift and souvenir shop on site
Facilities: National Park Information Point

Open: Daily; April to October, 10:00 am onwards.
Winter months - weekends and holidays - not
Christmas Day, 10:00 am onwards.
Charges: Admission charges apply
Description:
- A natural dry passage formed some 500,000 years ago with a superb collection of stalactites and stalagmites. Found by lead miners in the 19th century and now opened as a show cave.
- A video is shown after the cave visit.
- Animal remains discovered in the cave are on display in the Visitor Centre.

Grassington
Upper Wharfedale Folk Museum
Theme: Museum
Address: The Square, Grassington, N. Yorks, BD23 5AQ
Disabled: Wheelchair access to ground floor only.
Facilities: Parking, toilets, refreshments, shops and Yorkshire Dales National Park Centre available locally.
Open:
- April 1st to September 30th:- daily 2.00 to 4.30pm
- October 1st to March 31st: Saturday and Sunday only 2.00 to 4.30pm

Charges:
- Adults: 60p • Children/Concessions: 50p • Family: £2.00

Description: An 18th century Yorkshire Dales cottage, farming, geology, archaeology, lead mining and items of local interest
• Lead Mining • Minerals • Craft Tools • Lathes
• Dales Farming • Period Costumes • Folk Lore • Days of the Railway recalled • World War II Memorabilia •

Great Ayton
All Saints Church
Theme: Church or Church Ruins
Directions: Low Green, Great Ayton, N. Yorks.
Contact: Mr. R. J. Arkell
Tel: 01642 722 173
Open:
- April to October: Daily: 2.00 pm to 4.30 pm
- Also Tuesdays: 10.30 am to 12.30 pm

Charges: Admission FREE - Donations welcome
Description: Church where the famous explorer, Captain James Cook, worshipped as a boy. The Cook family grave is in the churchyard. Much of the original 12th Century fabric of the church remains today.

Great Ayton
Captain Cook's Monument

Theme : Monument
Directions: Easby Moor above Great Ayton
Description: 60ft high obelisk erected in 1827 as a memorial to the explorer. Born nearby in 1728, the son of a farm labourer, Cook explored the world from Antarctica to Alaska before being killed in Hawaii.

Great Ayton
Captain Cook Schoolroom Museum

Theme: Museum
Address: 101, High Street, Great Ayton, TS9 6NB
Tel: 01642 724296 01642 723358
Description: It was here, between 1736 and 1740, that Captain James Cook received his early education.

Great Ayton
James Cook's Cottage. Site of

Theme: Historic Site
Directions: Easby Lane, Great Ayton
Description: Granite memorial marking the site in Easby Lane of Cook's cottage, after it was dismantled and shipped to Australia in 1934.

Great Ayton
James Cook Sculpture

Theme: Statue or sculpture
Directions: High Green, Great Ayton
Description: Shows James at the age of 16, when he left Great Ayton to go to Staithes. Sculpted by Nicholas Dimbleby.

Great Ayton
Roseberry Topping

Theme: Scenic View, Walk or Ride
Directions: 2 miles north east of Great Ayton on A173
Tel: 01723 870 423
Description: National Trust property. Rises to 320m (1,057ft) and was once sacred to the Norse god Odin - the "God of War". 360 degree view from the summit.

Halifax
Bankfield Museum

Theme: Museum
Address: Boothtown Road, Halifax, HX3 6HG

Tel: 01422 354 823
Description: An impressive collection of textiles, historic, contemporary and from around the world.

Halifax
Eureka! The Museum for Children
Theme: Museum
Directions: Next to Halifax Railway Station.
Tel: 07626 983 191
www: www.eureka.org.uk
Description: The only hands-on museum in the UK designed and built specially for 3 - 12 year old children.

Halifax
Piece Hall
Theme: Arts Gallery or Centre
Address: Piece Hall, Halifax, HX1 1RE
Tel: 01422 344040
Description: One of the most significant and complete Georgian buildings in Britain. It was first opened on January 1st, 1779, as a market place for 'pieces' (hence the name) of woollen and worsted cloth made by the handloom weavers in the area around Halifax.

Halifax
Piece Hall Art Gallery
Theme: Arts Gallery or Centre
Directions: The gallery is situated in the Piece Hall.
Tel: 01422 358087
Description: It holds up to 8 temporary exhibitions each year, including art, craft, photography and design.

Halifax
Shibden Hall
Theme: House or House & Garden
Directions: 2 miles fromHalifax on the A58 Leeds road.
Tel: 01422 352 246
Description: First built in about 1420 many generations of people have lived and worked here. The rooms and displays are set out as if someone has just slipped out and may return at any moment

Harrogate
www: www.harrogate.gov.uk/tourism
Description: One of the most attractive towns and winner of 'Britain in Bloom' competition Harrogate has acres of immaculate gardens with an array of colour throughout the year, open spaces, elegant architecture and broad tree-lined boulevards. Following the

discovery of the first mineral water in 1571, the town evolved as a spa, ranking among the finest in the world.

Dignified Victorian buildings, with cast-iron canopies and cascading floral baskets, quality shops, hotels, restaurants and tea rooms.

Attractions include the **RHS Garden Harlow Carr** (p46), the **Valley Gardens** and the **Montpelier Gardens**.

The Tourist Information Centre is at Royal Baths, Crescent Road, Harrogate, Tel: 01423 537300. **www.harrogate.gov.uk/tourism**

Harrogate
Bettys Café Tea Rooms
Theme: Refreshments
Address: 1 Parliament Street, Harrogate
Tel: 01423 502746
Description: Also at Ilkley, Northallerton and York. For a fuller description see our entry under "York" (p123).

Harrogate (Summerbridge)
Brimham Rocks
Theme: Scenic View, Walk or Ride
Directions: 8 miles SW of Ripon, off B6265. 10 miles NW of Harrogate off B6165 road.
Description: A National Trust property. Spectacular views; moorland filled with strange and fantastic rock formations of millstone grit and rich in wildlife.

Harrogate
Darley Mill Centre
Theme: Shopping
Directions: 7 miles from Harrogate off the A59 and 2 miles from Pateley Bridge off the B6451 road.
Tel: 01423 780 857
Description: Great day out combining mill shopping with lots for the children to see and do.

Harrogate
Montpellier Gardens
Theme: Garden or Gardens
Description: A delightful floral area in the centre of town running the length of Montpellier Parade, one of the exclusive shopping streets in Harrogate.

Harrogate
RHS Garden Harlow Carr

Theme: Garden(s)
Directions: 1.5 miles from
Harrogate on the B6162
Otley Road.
Tel: 01423 565 418
**E-mail: admin-harlowcarr
@rhs.org.uk**
www: www.rhs.org.uk
Children: Welcome.
Disabled: Parking available.
Motorised & push
wheelchairs, booking
advisable.
Dogs: Registered assistant dogs only.
Parking: Free parking on site.
Toilets: Toilets on site.
Refreshments: Refreshments on site.
Open: 2003:
Gardens: every day of the year (including Christmas
and New Year) 9:30am to 6pm (dusk if earlier).
Plant Centre & Gift Shop: April to October 9:30am to
6pm; Sundays 11am to 5pm. November to March
9:30am to 5:30pm; Sundays 11am to 5pm. Call 01423
501809 for details.
Garden Room Café Bar and Restaurant: Snacks and
refreshments are served in the Café Bar every day from
9:30am to 5:30pm (10am-4pm Nov-Feb inclusive).
Restaurant is open for bookings only, call 01423
505604 for details.
Museum of Gardening: Shop hours
Charges:
Adults: £4.50, Senior Citizens: £4.00, Parties of over 20:
£3.50. Students: £2.00. Children under 11: free.
Children 11 to 16: £1.00. Children accompanying a
member: free.
Description:
Opened in 1950 as a trial ground to assess the
suitability of plants for growing in the northern climates.
The 58 acre RHS garden has ambitious plans for
development, whilst retaining the natural and 'informal'
style that is characteristic of Harlow Carr.

The Woodland and Arboretum are havens for wildlife
whilst the spectacular summer swathe of candelabra
primulas along the famous streamside will delight adults
and children alike. With scented, herb and foliage
gardens, the extensive vegetable, fruit and flower trails,
contemporary grasses border and much more, the keen
gardener or those just wanting a relaxing day out will
find Harlow Carr a place of magic and beauty.

Museum of Gardening and Library, Model Village, children's play area and picnic areas. Fully licensed café bar, plant centre, gift & bookshop. Coach Park. Advance booking for groups is preferable.

Harrogate
Royal Pump Room Museum
Theme: Museum
Directions: Easy walk from town centre.
Tel: 01423 556188
Description: Stands over Harrogate's famous sulphur wells, and still serves the strongest sulphur water in Europe. Museum recalls the elegance of a bygone era.

Hawes
Facilities: Car parking and toilets are available at the National Park Centre car park.
Description: At the head of Wensleydale, a busy market town with high fells to both the north and south. A cobbled main street and stone buildings that date from late Victorian times mingle with houses of the 17th and 18th centuries. ● The Dales Countryside Museum displays the history of the Dales and the traditional countryside way of life. Artefacts from agriculture to lead mining to the home front are on display. ● The Hawes Ropeworks gives a fascinating glimpse at a little known industry. ● The region's broad valleys with their lush green hills present ideal conditions for dairy farming, and Hawes is the home of the famous Wensleydale Cheese. The small museum explains the process of cheesemaking topped off with a tour of the creamery where the cheese is made. ● The dramatic drive over Buttertubs Pass, a natural pass whose limestone formations are said to resemble butter, is just north of the village. ● There is a Tourist Information Centre at the Dales Countryside Museum. Tel: 01969 667 450

Hawes
Buttertubs Pass
Theme: Scenic View, Walk or Ride
Description: Well known scenic drive from Wensleydale into Swaledale, one of the highest stretches of road in the country. Derives its name from a series of deep limestone shafts.

Hawes
Dales Countryside Museum

Theme: Museum (and Information Centre)
Directions: Station Yard, Hawes, just off the A684 at the Eastern end of the town.
Tel: 01969 667 450
E-mail: dcm@yorkshiredales.org.uk
www: www.destinationdales.org.uk
Children: Baby changing facility, FREE entry
Disabled: Access for wheelchair users
Dogs: Only guidedogs in museum
Parking: Parking on site
Toilets: Toilets on site
Open: Daily 10:00am to 5:00pm except Christmas and New Year holidays.
Charges: Information Centre – FREE entry • Museum – admission charge applies but FREE for children.
Description: Housed in old railway station buildings in the heart of the National Park, the Dales Countryside Museum is the ideal place to start your visit to the Yorkshire Dales. The Museum tells the story of the people and places in this special area and brings alive the past of the Dales. • Hands-on displays, gallery gotcha drop in events, exhibitions and demonstrations. Also shop and Tourist Information and National Park Centre.

Hawes
Hawes Ropemaker

Theme: Craft Workshop and shop
Speciality: Traditional ropemaking
Directions: On A684 at junction with access road to Dales Countryside Museum.
Tel: 01969 667 487
E-mail: sales@ropemakers.com
www: www.ropemakers.com
Disabled: Wheelchair walkway (Monday to Friday).
Parking: Parking adjacent.
Open: Open all year.
* Monday to Friday 9:00am to 5:30pm except Christmas & Good Friday.

- July to October also open Saturdays 10:00am to 5:00pm.

Charges: Admission free. Ropeworks book £1.00
Description: Watch traditional ropemaking and see how the twist is put in. Dog leads, bannister ropes, clothes lines and many more items in our well stocked shop.

Hawes
Wensleydale Creamery

Theme: Visitor Centre
Address: Gayle Lane, Hawes, N. Yorks, DL8 3RN
Tel: 01969 667 664
Description: Home of the famous "Wensleydale" cheese. Exhibition, demonstrations, Cheese Shop etc.

Haworth

Description: Situated on the edge of the Pennine Moors with a steep Main Street, paved with stone setts and lined with historic inns, shops, galleries and cafés, leading down to one of Britain's best preserved steam railways.

- More than a century ago the Reverend Patrick Brontë came to be a minister at Haworth Parish Church. Within a few decades, a series of books written by Charlotte, Emily and Anne, caused this obscure Yorkshire village to become a major centre for literary pilgrimage.
- The spirit of the Brontës lives on and few can leave Haworth without sensing it. Visitors can tour the Georgian **Brontë Parsonage Museum**, home to the Brontës, which contains a vast collection of their artefacts and see the village church, where most of their family are buried.
- Take a trip back in time riding on the **Keighley and Worth Valley Railway** where such films as The Railway Children and Yanks were made, or experience one of the special vintage trains or Thomas the Tank Engine weekends.
- There are many good tea rooms, souvenir and antiquarian bookshops, restaurants, pubs and hotels (including the "Black Bull" - where Branwell Brontë's demise into alcoholism and opium addiction allegedly began). The **Brontë Weaving Shed** stocks a superb range of knitwear and clothing for all the family, an amazing range of gifts and souvenirs and the latest range of speciality Yorkshire foods and confectionery. **Ponden Mill** is a "Bargain Hunter's Paradise" or you may dare to join the **Lanternlight Graveyard Tour** after dark to savour where almost 40,000 souls lie.

Haworth
Brontë Parsonage Museum

Theme: Museum

Directions: Haworth. Just off the A6033 about 2 miles south of Keighley.

Address: Haworth, Keighley, West Yorkshire, BD22 8DR

Tel: 01535 642 323 **Fax:** 01535 647 131

E-mail: bronte@bronte.org.uk

www: www.bronte.info

Children: Are welcome

Dogs: Regret dogs not allowed, except guide dogs.

Parking: Public parking nearby.

Shop: A comprehensive stock of books by and about the Brontës and a wide range of souvenirs.

Open:

- April to September Daily 10.00am. Last admission 5.00pm
- October to March Daily 11.00am to 4.30pm

Charges:

- Adult - £4.80 • Child (5-6 incusive) - £1.50
- Family Ticket - £10.50 (two adults and up to three children) • Student/Senior Citizen - £3.50

Description: An extraordinary literary family. The Rev. Patrick Brontë, his wife Maria and their six children came to the Parsonage in 1820. The eldest girls, Maria and Elizabeth died here in infancy but Charlotte, Branwell, Emily and Anne survived to adulthood. • They went on to write - Emily's Wuthering Heights in 1847, Charlotte's Jane Eyre in 1847 and Anne's The Tenant of Wildfell Hall in 1848. ●

The Brontës were an intensely close-knit family and their Parsonage home formed the heart of their world from early childhood until the ends of their brief lives, whilst the Yorkshire moorland setting provided them with inspiration for their writing. ●

The Parsonage, built in 1778/9, is set out with the Brontës' own furniture and possessions, bringing the rooms to life as they would have been at the time the family lived there. It houses a unique collection of personal treasures, pictures, clothes and manuscripts; including the world famous 'little books' the Brontës produced as children, Branwell's striking portraits of local people and a changing display of Charlotte's tiny dresses, bonnets and shoes. There are also permanent and temporary exhibition spaces interpreting various aspects of the Brontës' lives and works.

Haworth
Brontë Weaving Shed

Theme: Visitor Centre
Directions: The Brontë Weaving Shed is at Townend Mill, Haworth.
Tel: 01535 646 217
Children: Well behaved children are always welcome, they will love our "Timmy Feather Weaving Exhibition".
Disabled: The whole of the Mill is on one level, with space for wheelchair access.

Dogs: Well behaved dogs on leads are welcome.
Parking: Large pay and display car park opposite the Mill.
Toilets: Free toilets on site.
Refreshments: Over 20 places to eat and drink in nearby Haworth Village just 5 minutes walk away.
Open: We are open 7 days

per week, all year.
Description: One of Haworth's main attractions.

- An impressive water wheel turns all day creating a picture of how power and industry used to be here in West Yorkshire.
- The Brontë Weaving Shed contains an exhibition in the form of a tribute to Timmy Feather - the last of Yorkshire's Handloom Weavers. It contains a fully working Victorian Handloom still used to this day to create the famous Brontë Tweed.
- Available most afternoons from April to December, you are invited to come along and hear "The Weavers Tale" your opportunity to meet our resident weaver, discover the full story from fleece to piece, try your hand at weaving and take home a free souvenir piece of Brontë Tweed.
- Take time to browse through the superb range of knitwear and clothing for all the family, an amazing range of gifts and souvenirs and our latest range of speciality Yorkshire foods, confectionery and ales. Why not sample some of Scotland's finest malts in our new beer and whisky shop.

Haworth
Lanternlight Graveyard Tour

Theme: Guided Tour
Directions: Meet at The Old
Stocks, Haworth village.
Tel: 01535 642 329
Children: Suitable for children
over 10 years.
Refreshments: Tickets include
discounts on late suppers
available in Haworth village.
Open: Tours available at 8:00 pm
every Saturday night during April,
May, September, October, November and December.
Special tours available Halloween Week!
Charges: Tours available by Ticket only, Adults £5.00,
Children £3.00. Lanterns provided. Bookings at
Haworth Tourist Information Centre, telephone credit
card booking service available.
Description: During the darker months of the year,
when the locals have retired behind locked and bolted
doors dare you join your guide to explore by
Lanternlight the Graveyard believed to house almost
40,000 souls • Lasting a bone chilling 60 minutes the
Tours have featured on Radio and Television. Private
Group bookings for 15+ are available on alternative
nights.

Haworth
Ponden Mill

Theme: Shopping
Directions: Colne Road, Stanbury
Tel: 01535 643 500
Description: One of the most famous textile mills in the
North of England, piled high with thousands of bargains.

Hebden Bridge
Hardcastle Crags

Theme: Scenic View, Walk or Ride
Directions: 1 • miles North of Hebden Bridge
Tel: 01422 844 518
Description: Beautiful wooded valley with deep rocky
ravines, tumbling streams and woodland rich in natural
history. Waymarked walks past 19th century cotton mill.

Helmsley
Duncombe Park

Theme: House & Garden
Directions: 25 miles north of York off the A170 Thirsk - Scarborough road, 1 mile from Helmsley marketplace.
Tel: 01439 770 213
E-mail: sally@duncombepark.com
www: www.duncombepark.com
Children: Quizzes available for House & gardens. Orienteering, Small playground. Regretably pushchairs are not allowed in the house.
Disabled: Most areas are user friendly with a unisex toilet for the disabled at the Parkland Centre.
Dogs: Allowed in the parkland only on a lead.
Parking: Parking on site.
Toilets: Toilets on site.
Refreshments: Parkland Tea Room.
Open: 22nd April to Sunday 26th October, 2003 (Sunday to Thursday).
- **House** (by guided tour only):
- 12:00 noon to 5:00 pm. - Tours hourly at half past the hour 12:30 pm to 3:30 pm.
- **Gardens, Parkland Centre Tearoom and Shop and Parkland Walks**:
- 11:00 am to 5:30 pm.

Last admission to gardens and parkland 4:30 pm.

Charges: 2003	House & Gardens	Gardens & Parkland	Parkland only
Adult	£6.00	£3.00	£2.00
Concession	£5.00	£3.00	
Child (10-16yrs)	£3.00	£1.50	£1.00
Groups (min 15)	£4.50	£2.75	

Description: Lord and Lady Feversham moved back to the ancestral home in 1986. They have undertaken extensive restoration of the buildings and interiors. The family pictures and Lord Feversham's collection of English and Continental furniture are on show and the principal rooms remain a fine example of the type of 'grand interior' popular at the turn of the century.

The early 18th century green gardens of 35 acres (14 hectares) have been described as "the supreme masterpiece of the art of the landscape gardener". Explore the great lawn and level terraces, temples, yew tree walk, woodland walks and the 'scented' garden around the old conservatory.

Helmsley
Helmsley Castle

Theme: Castle or Castle Ruins
Directions: Near to the town centre
Tel: 01439 770 442
Description: An English Heritage property. Beyond magnificent double earth works there is a spectacular 12th century fortress.

Helmsley
Helmsley Walled Garden

Theme: Garden or Gardens
Directions: Near to the town centre
Tel: 01439 771 427
www: www.helmsleywalledgarden.co.uk
Description: Beautiful 5 acre walled garden set against the spectacular backdrop of **Helmsley Castle** in the grounds of **Duncombe Park**.

Helmsley
Rievaulx Abbey

Theme: Abbey or Abbey Ruins
Directions: 2$\frac{1}{2}$ miles NW of Helmsley on B1257
Tel: 01439 798 228.
Description: An English Heritage property. One of the most impressive of monastic sites. These silent stones are the shell of the first Cistercian monastery in the North.

Helmsley
Rievaulx Terrace and Temples

Theme: Abbey or Abbey Ruins
Directions: 2$\frac{1}{2}$ miles NW of Helmsley on B1257
Tel: 01439 798 340
Description: A National Trust Property. Half mile grass covered terrace with adjoining woodlands, offering classic vistas over Rievaulx Abbey (English Heritage) and the rolling landscape of the Hambleton Hills.

Helmsley
Spout House

Theme: Historic Building
Directions: 8 miles North of Helmsley on the B1257 road in Bilsdale. Adjacent to the Sun Inn.
Description: A remarkably well preserved example of a thatched 16th century cruck-framed house. Renovated in 1982.

Hornsea
Freeport Hornsea Retail and Leisure Village
Theme: Shopping
Address: Rolston Road, Hornsea, E. Yorks, HU18 1UT
Tel: 01964-534211 01964-536363
www: www.freeportplc.com
Description: Big name fashion brands to kitchenware & china at up to 50% off high street prices.

Hornsea
Hornsea Museum
Theme: Museum (Folk)
Address: Burns Farm, 11, Newbegin, Hornsea.
Tel: 01964 533 443
www: www.hornseamuseum.com
Description: Sited in an 18th Century farmhouse home of the Burn family for 300 years. Rooms show how the Burns lived, worked and played 100 years ago.

Huddersfield
Kirklees Light Railway
Theme: Scenic Steam Railway
Directions: A 636 Wakefield to Denby Dale Road. 4 miles from M1 – Junction 39 from North; Junction 38 from South. Near to Huddersfield, Barnsley & Wakefield
Address: Park Mill Way, Clayton West, Huddersfield, West Yorks, HD8 9XJ
Tel: 01484 865 727
www: www.kirkleeslightrailway.com
Children: Welcome.
Disabled: Welcome.
Parking: Ample FREE parking.
Refreshments: Large café.
Shop: Souvenirs and toys.
Open: All weekends, most school holidays and every day from Spring Bank Holiday to 1st September. Hourly trains from 11am to 4pm summer (3pm winter).
Charges: Fares ● **Adults**:- £5.50 ● **OAP**:- £5 ● **Child 3-15 years**:- £3.50 ● **Family Ticket (2 + 2)**:- £16
Events: Exciting Special Events programme includes **"Day Out With Thomas"** weekends in June and July.
Description: 50 minute scenic ride on **YORKSHIRE'S GREAT LITTLE STEAM TRAIN** through the lovely South Pennines on an old country branch line.

Hull
Arctic Corsair
Theme: Museum (Maritime)

Directions: Access is via Wilberforce House Museum.
Tel: 01482 613 902
Description: The last of the Hull 'side-winder' fishing vessels. The Arctic Corsair has been fully restored.

Hull (Sproatley)
Burton Constable Hall

Theme: House or House & Garden
Directions: From Beverley (14 miles) follow the A165 Bridlington road and from Hull (7miles) follow the B1238 to the village of Sproatley. The route to the hall is clearly marked by historic house signs.

Address: The Burton Constable Foundation, Burton Constable, East Yorkshire, HU11 4LN
Tel: 01964 562400
Fax: 01964 563229
E-mail: enquiries@burtonconstable.com
www: www.burtonconstable.com
Disabled: Car parking is available at the front of the Hall. Other facilities include a stairlift to the first floor.
Dogs: On lead only.
Parking: Free car parking. All toilet facilties are situated in the Stable Block in the corner of the car park.
Refreshments: The Tea Room is open at 12.30 p.m., serving a range of light refreshments, afternoon teas, etc. Group menus are available.
Shop: Small gift shop.
Open:
- Easter Sunday to the end of October, Saturday to Thursday inclusive.
- The Hall is open 1.00 p.m. to 5.00 p.m. (Last admission 4.00pm)
- The Grounds and Tea Room from 12.30 p.m. to 5.00 p.m.

Charges: Adults: £5.00 ● **OAP**: £4.50 ● **Child**: £2.00 ● **Family** (2 Adults + up to 4 children): £11.00 ● **Groups** (20+): £4.00
Description: Burton Constable was built during the reign of Queen Elizabeth I. Superb 18th and 19th century interiors of faded grandeur including a Gallery, Great Hall, Dining and Drawing Rooms, Bedrooms, Chapel, Chinese Room, Museum of Natural Curiosities and fascinating Lamp Room. Outside the house there are gardens with statues, an orangery, stable block and wildfowl lakes set in 300 acres of parkland landscaped by 'Capability' Brown.

Hull
Ferens Art Gallery
Theme: Arts Gallery or Centre
Address: Queen Victoria Square, HU1 3RA
Description: Internationally renowned permanent
collection and programmes of exhibitions and Live Art.

Hull
Fort Paull
Theme: Museum (Military & Armouries)
Directions: On the A1033, East from Hull's Hedon
Road (Saltend roundabout) through Paull.
Tel: 01482 89 3339
Description: Has played an important role in the
defence of Britain since the time of Henry VIII. A series
of displays & exhibits capture different periods of history

Hull
Hands on History
Theme: Museum
Address: South Church Side, Hull, HU1 1RR
Tel: 01482 613902
Description: "Victorian Britain", the "Story of Hull and
its People" and "Ancient Egypt".

Hull
Hull & East Riding Museum
Theme: Museum
Address: High Street, Hull, HU1 1PS
Tel: 01482 613 902.
Description: 70 million years of history Dinosaurs,
Roman Gallery, Celtic World, Undersea Dome.

Hull
Maritime Museum
Theme: Museum
Address: Queen Victoria Square, Hull, HU1 3DX
Description: Hull's rich and colourful maritime history.
Fine collection of paintings, artefacts and models.

Hull
Spurn Lightship
Theme: Maritime History
Address: Spurn Lightship, Hull Marina, Hull.
Description: The 'Spurn' served for 48 years as a vital
navigation aid in the approaches to the river Humber.

Hull
Streetlife

Theme: Museum (Transport)
Address: High Street, Hull, HU1 1PS
Description: Motor car gallery, extended carriage gallery, larger street-scene with several new shops.

Hull
The Deep

Theme: Aquarium
Directions: Within walking distance from the City Centre on the bank of the River Humber.
Tel: 01482 381 000
www: www.thedeep.co.uk
Description: Dramatic fusion of aquaria and state of the art interactives telling the story of the world's oceans through time, latitude and depth.

Hull
Wilberforce House

Theme: Museum
Address: 25 High Street, Hull HU1 1NQ
Tel: 01482 6123 902
Description: The main displays tell the horrific story of slavery and Wilberforce's fight to abolish it.

Ilkley

www: www.visitilkley.com
Description: Situated in the Wharfe Valley, this spa town is surrounded by glorious countryside. The southern slopes form Ilkley Moor, immortalised in Yorkshire's anthem—"On Ilkla Moor Baht 'at". • Prehistoric man lived on the moors and left behind stone circles and hundreds of rock carvings, including the famous Swastika Stone. • The town centre has an unhurried atmosphere with tree-lined avenues, select shops and excellent restaurants, elegant hotels and comfortable guest houses. • On the northern slopes of the valley lie Middleton Woods, well worth a visit at any time, but especially in May when the bluebells are spectacular.

Ilkley
Bettys Café Tea Rooms

Theme: Refreshments
Address: 32 The Grove
Tel: 01943 608029
Description: Also at Harrogate, Northallerton and York. For a fuller description see our entry under "York" (p123).

Ilkley
Ilkley Toy Museum

Theme: Museum
Address: Whitton Croft Road, Ilkley, LS29 9HR
Tel: 01943 603855
Fax: 01943 602043
E-mail: ilkleytoymuseum@supanet.com
www: www.ilkleytoymuseum.co.uk or
www.visitbradford.com/attractions.asp
Children: Very welcome. Free quiz with prize.
Disabled: Wheelchair ramp to front door. Full ground
floor access. (Stairs to
first floor) Disabled toilet.
Dogs: Guide dogs only.
Parking: On street
parking (free) or pay and
display in Ilkley central
car park.

Toilets: Available on site.
Shop: Small gift shop.
Open: All year round.
Opening hours will be
increased to some
weekdays in school
holidays. Please ring for
up to date information.

- Saturday: 12.00pm - 4.00pm
- Sunday & Bank Holidays: 12.00pm - 4.00pm

Charges:
- Adult: £3
- Child: (5-16 years)   £2
- Child under 5:   Free
- Family ticket (2 Adults & 3 children):   £8

Description: The museum contains one of the finest
private collections of toys in
the North of England with a
particularly fine display of
early English wooden dolls.
The many exhibits feature
dolls, dolls houses, teddy
bears, tin plate toys, lead
figures and a selection of
games together with
wooden and paper toys.
Dating from 350BC to the

present day the exhibits include a 1940's English
working model fairground.

Ilkley
Manor House Art Gallery and Museum

Theme: Arts Gallery or Centre
Address: Castle Yard, Ilkley, LS29 9DT
Tel: 01943 600066
www.bradford.gov.uk/tourism/museums
Description: Stands on part of the site of Roman fort of Olicana. Local history, Roman remains and art gallery.

Ilkley
White Wells

Theme: Health Spa or Centre
Address: Spa Cottage, Ilkley Moor, Ilkley, LS29 9RF
Tel: 01943 608035
Description: Spring Water Bath and Well famous for its healing, in the beautiful setting of Ilkley Moor.

Ingleton

www: www.ingleton.co.uk
Parking: At the National Park Centre car park.
Description: A picturesque market town surrounded by natural wonders. Ideal base for lovely walks and for the "Three Peaks" of Ingleborough (p35), Pen-y-ghent (p109) and Whernside (p61). Surrounded by magnificent countryside with caves, waterfalls, and mountains. The Craven Fault crosses the area, and geological and archaeological sites abound.
Local attractions include: ● White Scar Cave, Britain's largest show cave • Waterfalls Walk through woodland gorges with spectacular waterfalls. ● Nearby Settle-Carlisle railway and the famous Ribblehead viaduct

Ingleton
Country Harvest

Theme: Shopping
Directions: On the A-65 at Ingleton.
Tel: 015242 42223
Description: Quality local produce and gifts alongside goods from further afield.

Ingleton
Daleswear Factory Shop

Theme: Shopping
Address: Laundry Lane, Ingleton, N. Yorks,LA6 3DF
Tel: 01524 242 373 **Fax:** 01524 241 047
Description: Outdoor and leisurewear. Portalec fleeces, waterproof clothing and caving gear.

Ingleton
Ingleton Waterfalls Walk

Theme: Scenic View, Walk or Ride
Directions: Signposted from the main roads.
Tel: 01524 241 930
Description: Lovely 4$^1/_2$ circular mile walk via Thornton Force, Rival Falls, Baxenghyll Gorge and Snow Falls.

Ingleton
Whernside

Theme: Land or Seascape
Description: Highest point in the Dales, reaching to 2,415 feet (736m) and as such the highest of the "Three Peaks" (see also Ingleborough (p35) and Pen-y-ghent (p109)). ● It has a less dramatic millstone grit summit than its two cousins but it is often termed the 'roof' of Yorkshire. ● There are several approaches to Whernside, but the two most popular are from the Ribblehead Viaduct or from Chapel-le-Dale. ● Trains from nearby Horton-in-Ribblesdale can be seen crossing the viaduct at Ribblehead to disappear into Blea Moor whilst Pen-y-ghent (p109) and Ingleborough (p35) are to the east and south.

Ingleton
White Scar Cave

Theme: Cave or Caves
Directions: 1$^1/_2$ miles North of Ingleton on the B6255.
Tel: 01524 241 244 **Fax:** 01524 241 700
Description: Britain's longest show cave has been sculpted by nature over thousands of years.

Keighley
Cliffe Castle Museum

Theme: Museum
Address: Spring Gardens Lane, Keighley, BD20 6LH
Tel: 01535 618231 **Fax:** 01535 610536
Description: Displays of local fossils and geology, crystals and minerals, natural history, local bygones, stained glass, pottery and furnished Victorian rooms.

Keighley
East Riddlesden Hall

Theme: House & Garden
Directions: 1 mile NE of Keighley on B6265.
Tel: 01535 607 075
Description: A National Trust Property. This homely merchant's house and garden has stood at the heart of Riddlesden, Keighley, for over 600 years.

Keighley
Keighley and Worth Valley Railway

Theme: Scenic Railway
Directions: South Street, Keighley
Tel: 01535 645 214
Description: Branch line from Keighley to the Brontës and beyond. Operated by volunteers since 1968.

Keighley
Keighley Bus Museum

Theme: Museum
Address: Old Dalton Lane, Keighley.
Tel: 01282 413179
Description: A collection of over fifty buses and coaches dating from 1927 to the late 1970's.

Keighley
Vintage Carriages Trust Museum of Rail Travel

Theme: Museum
Address: Railway Station, Keighley, BD22 8NJ
Tel: 01535 680425
Description: Fascinating award winning collection of railway vehicles.

Kirkbymoorside
Farndale

Theme: Scenic View, Walk or Ride
Directions: Access from East of Kirkbymoorside.
Description: Renowned for its daffodil walk. From Low Mill Car Park follow the clearly marked footpath alongside the River Dove to Church Houses. Usually at its best during the 3rd and 4th weeks in April each year.

Kirkbymoorside (Hutton-le-Hole)
Ryedale Folk Museum

Theme: Museum
Directions: Signposted from A170 road between Kirkbymoorside and Pickering.
Address: Hutton-le-Hole, York, N. Yorks, YO62 6UA
Tel: 01751 417 367 **Fax:** 01751 417 367
Description: Rescued and restored buildings chart the changes in rural life.

Knaresborough

Description: Picturesque market town with breathtaking views over the River Nidd. Georgian Houses, narrow streets and a maze of alleys and ginnels, boating and pleasant riverside walks.

Knaresborough
Bebra Gardens

Theme: Garden or Gardens
Description: Named after Knaresborough's twin town in Germany. Flower beds, luxuriant lawns; open daily.

Knaresborough
Conyngham Hall Grounds

Theme: Park or Garden(s)
Description: Tennis courts, pitch and putt, woodland and riverside walks. Boating facilities close by.

Knaresborough
Henshaws Arts & Crafts Centre

Theme: Arts Gallery or Centre
Address: Bond End, Knaresborough, HG5 9AL
Tel: 01423 541 888
www: www.knaresborough.co.uk/henshaws/
Description: Displays many pieces of commissioned art work. Craftshops open to the public.

Knaresborough
Knaresborough Castle & Museum

Theme: Castle or Castle Ruins
Directions: Easy walk from the town centre.
Tel: 01423 866 886 01423 556188
Description: Castle stands on a cliff high above the River Nidd. First built in about 1100 and almost completely rebuilt by Edward I in the early 14th century. Museum tells the story of the town's long history.

Knaresborough
Mother Shipton's Cave and The Petrifying Well

Theme: Historic Place
Directions: On the A59 4 miles east of Harrogate.
Tel: 01423 864 600
Description: England's most famous Prophetess. Born in 1488 just a few feet from the famous Petrifying Well.

Leeds

Description: Second largest metropolitan district in the UK of which two thirds is Green Belt - affording some of the most beautiful scenery in Yorkshire. ● A vibrant, affluent capital complementing its economic success with a lively arts, sporting and entertainment scene. New and refurbished theatres, shopping malls, hotels, galleries and café bars rub shoulders with stylish offices and award-winning architecture. ● Visitor attractions especially worthy of a visit include the **Armley Mills Industrial Museum, Harewood House and Bird Garden**, the **Henry Moore Institute**, the **Horsforth Village Museum of Local History** , **Kirkstall Abbey, Leeds City Art Gallery, Middleton Railway**, the **Royal Armouries**, the **Thackray Medical Museum** and the **York Gate Garden**.

The Tourist Information Centre is at Leeds City Station. Tel 0113 242 5242, **tourinfo@leeds.gov.uk** or **www.leeds.gov.uk**

Leeds
Abbey House Museum
Theme: Museum
Address: Kirkstall Road, Leeds,
Tel: 0113 230 5492
Description: Walk the re-created Victorian streets and shops and houses of old-time Leeds around 1880.

Leeds
Armley Mills, Leeds Industrial Museum
Theme: Museum
Directions: 2 miles West of City Centre off the A65.
Tel: 0113 263 7861
Description: Once the world's largest woollen mill, is now an award-winning industrial museum.

Leeds
City Art Gallery
Theme: Arts Gallery or Centre
Address: The Headrow, Leeds LS1 3AA
Tel: 0113 247 8248
Description: Internationally acclaimed collection of works on paper and a modern sculpture collection.

Leeds
Emsley's Farm Shop & Visitor Centre
Theme: Farm, Farm Visitor Centre or Farm Shop
Address: Greenside Farm, Warm Lane, Yeadon,
Tel: 0113 250 3060 **Fax:** 0113 239 1485
Description: Fresh Farm Eggs, Milk & Local Produce. Pets Corner, Bouncy Castle, Gardeners Corner etc.

Leeds
Harewood House and Bird Garden
Theme: House & Garden

HAREWOOD
VISITOR ATTRACTION OF THE YEAR
WHITE ROSE AWARDS 2002

Directions: 7 miles from Leeds & Harrogate on the A61
Tel: 0113 218 1010
E-mail: business@harewood.org
www: www.harewood.org
Children: Welcome. The resemblance in summer of The Adventure Playground to an animated ant-heap testifies to its popularity.
Disabled: Most areas are wheelchair accessible.
Facilities: Parking, toilets, refreshments and shop.
Awards: Yorkshire Tourist Board Visitor Attraction of the Year.
Events: Most Sundays as well as Theatre and Concerts on some evenings.
Open: House, Grounds and Bird Garden March to end of October then Grounds Winter Weekends to mid December.
Description: Exquisite House interiors, royal memorabilia, changing art exhibitions, fascinating old kitchen, stunning scenery, premier Bird Garden and thrilling adventure playground.

Leeds
Henry Moore Institute
Theme: Sculpture Gallery
Directions: Adjacent to the City Art Gallery. 5 minutes walk from Leeds Station.
Address: 74 The Headrow, Leeds, LS1 3AH
Tel: Information line: (0113) 234 3158
Fax: Fax: (0113) 246 1481

www: www.henry-moore-fdn.co.uk
Disabled: Disabled access at side of building via Cookridge Street entrance. Parking in Cookridge Street. Braille information available at reception.
Open:
- Mon-Sun 10am-5.30pm,
- Wed 10am-9pm.
- Closed bank holidays.

Charges: Admission is Free
Description: Part of the Henry Moore Foundation and supported by Leeds City Council. Aims are achieved through a programme of exhibitions, talks, lectures, conferences, academic fellowships, artist residencies, publications and collaborative projects.

Leeds (Horsforth)
Horsforth Village Museum of Local History

Theme: Museum
Address: The Green, Horsforth, Leeds, LS18 5JH
Tel: 0113 281 9877
www: www.leedscommunity.co.uk
Disabled: On ground floor only.
Facilities: There is parking nearby. The Museum shop sells souvenirs, stationary and books. Toilets available.
Open:
- Last Saturday in March to the end of December.
- Saturday 10.am - 4.00pm • Sunday 2.00pm - 5.00pm

Charges: Admission is FREE.
Description: Once described as the largest village in England Horsforth has managed to retain its identity, character and sense of community. The Museum reflects this heritage in its exhibits.

Leeds
Kirkstall Abbey

Abbey or Abbey Ruins
Directions: From City Centre take A65 for $2^1/_2$ miles.
www: www.leeds.gov.uk/kirkstallabbey
Description: One of Britain's best preserved abbeys, Founded in 1152. Closed down in November 1539.

Leeds (Aberford)
Lotherton Hall & Gardens

Theme: House or House & Garden
Directions: 13 miles north-east of Leeds city centre and one mile east of the A1 at Aberford on the B1217.
Tel: 0113 281 3259
Description: Edwardian gentleman's country residence housing the Gascoigne Gift of paintings, furniture, etc.

Leeds
Meanwood Valley Urban Farm
Theme: Farm, Farm Visitor Centre or Farm Shop
Directions: 1$\frac{1}{2}$ miles north of the centre of Leeds.
Tel: 0113 262 9759
Description: A selection of farm animals, rare breeds, organic market garden, nature area, bird feeding station & ponds. Visit the shop and lunch in the Café.

Leeds (Hunslet)
Middleton Railway
Theme: Rail Journey
Address: Moor Road, Hunslet, Leeds, LS10 2JQ
Tel: 0113 271 0320
www: www.middletonrailway.org.uk
Description: Opened in 1758 it was the world's first railway. Trains now carry passengers along a one mile route between Moor Road Hunslet and Middleton Park.

Leeds
Royal Armouries Museum
Theme : Museum
Directions: Well signed off Junction 4 of the M621
Tel: 0113 220 1999
www: www.armouries.org.uk
Description: Opened in 1996 as the new home for the national collection of arms and armour. Five themed galleries covering War, Tournament, Self-Defence, Hunting and the arms and armour of the Orient.

Leeds
Temple Newsam Home Farm
Theme: Farm, Farm Visitor Centre or Farm Shop
Address: Temple Newsam Estate, Leeds, LS15 OAD
Tel: 0113 264 5535
Description: Largest working Rare Breeds Centre in the county. Agricuitural museum. All set in 1500 acres of historic parkland, woodland and gardens.

Leeds
Temple Newsam House
Theme : House or House & Garden
Directions: 4 miles from Leeds city centre off the A63/M1 north, jncn 46.
Tel: 0113 264 7321
Description: Magnificent Tudor-Jacobean mansion in a 900 acre park laid out by Capability Brown. Birth-place of Lord Darnley, husband of Mary, Queen of Scots.

Leeds
Thackray Medical Museum
Theme : Museum
Directions: Follow signs St James's Hospital. Museum is 100 metres from hospital main entrance.
Tel: 0113 244 4343
www: www.thackraymuseum.org
Description: Award-winning interactive museum looks at the ways in which people's lives have changed over the last 150 years as a result of improved living conditions and medical advances.

Leeds (Stourton)
Thwaite Mills Watermill
Theme: Industrial History
Directions: 2 miles south of Leeds city centre off the A61. Half a mile from junction 43 off the M1
Tel: 0113 249 6453
Description: Fully restored working water-powered mill and museum of over 300 years of industry.

Leeds (Oakwood)
Tropical World
Theme: Garden or Gardens
Directions: 3 miles North of City Centre off the A58.
Tel: 0113 266 1850
Description: Home to the largest collection of tropical plants outside Kew Gardens.

Leeds
York Gate Garden
Theme: Garden or Gardens

Owner: Perennial – Gardeners' Royal Benevolent Society
Address: Back Church Lane, Adel, Leeds, LS16 8DW

PLACES OF INTEREST

Tel: 0113 267 8240
www: www.perennial.org.uk
Directions: *From Leeds* take the A660 for Otley. Right at the first set of traffic-lights after the ring road (A6120). Left into Church Lane and park near the Church. A public footpath through the churchyard and straight on passes the gate. *From the north*, take the A660 through Bramhope. Left at the first set of traffic-lights after the Ramada Jarvis Hotel. Left into Church Lane as above. **By Bus** - No. 28 From Leeds to Adel. Alight at Adel Wood Stores. Walk to the garden along Sir George Martin Drive. ● No.1 From Leeds to Holt Park. Alight near the traffic lights in Adel. Walk to the garden via Church Lane. ● No. X84 From Skipton to Leeds. Alight at Leeds-Holt Lane. Walk to the garden via Church Lane.
Disabled: Wheelchair access is limited.
Dogs: Not allowed in the garden (except guide dogs).
Parking: In Church Lane, near the Church.
Toilets: There are toilet facilities.
Refreshments: Tea, coffee and biscuits – June to September.
Open: April to September ● Thursdays, Sundays and Bank Holiday Mondays, 2 - 5 pm ● Evenings - June 26th and July 3rd, 6 - 9 pm
Charges: Admission is by donation to Perennial:- Adults £3.00 ● Children (16 and under) FREE. ● Coach parties welcome by appointment.
Description: One acre masterpiece renowned for its outstanding design and exquisite detail.

Created by the Spencer family between 1951 and 1994. Frederick Spencer laid down the basic structure of the garden but his son, Robin, was largely responsible for its development. His remarkable sense of perspective, clever use of materials and meticulous attention to detail led to the creation of one of the country's most inspirational small gardens. After his sudden death his mother, Sybil, nurtured the garden. A gifted plantswoman – she enhanced the diverse plant collection which remains today.

In just one acre, the garden contains shrub and herbaceous borders, ponds, topiary, a miniature pinetum, dell, nut walk, fern border, white garden, kitchen garden and famous herb garden with summer-house. Special features include a pavement maze, espaliered Cedar and Yew pyramids.

Leyburn
Beech End Model Village

Theme: Model Village
Directions: Across the square from the Bolton Arms and along an alley between shops.
Address: Commercial Square, Leyburn, N. Yorks, DL8 5BP
Contact: Ian or Adele Calvert
Tel: 01969 625400
E-mail: ian@beech-end.co.uk
www: www.beech-end.co.uk
Children: Great attraction from $2^{1}/_{2}$ upwards; see description below.
Disabled: The exhibit is on the first floor; gentle stairs but we regret no self-access for wheelchair visitors. Ring for individual information.
Shop: Ground floor shop stocked with gifts, novelties and toys.
Open: Easter to October
- School holiday weeks – daily 10.30am to 5pm;
- Other weeks – Sat & Sun 10.30am to 5pm; Mon, Wed & Fri 2pm to 5pm
- Ring to confirm (or see website) if travelling far.

Charges: Adults - £1.90 ● Senior citizens - £1.60
● Children under 14 - £1.30 ● Children under 3 - free
● No extra charge for operating models on the exhibit.
Description: A unique, interactive experience.
Our miniature village combines fascinating visual detail with interactive involvement – push button light & sound effects and working scale models, including boats on the picturesque canal and road vehicles.
Whatever your age you will find plenty to interest and entertain you. For a challenge why not try the quiz!

Leyburn
Bolton Castle

Theme: Castle or Castle Ruins
Address: Bolton Castle, Near Leyburn.
Tel: 01969 623 981
Description: With walls up to 9ft thick it has been dominating Wensleydale since 1379.

Leyburn
Constable Burton Hall Gardens

Theme: Garden(s)
Directions: Constable Burton; 8 miles west of the A1 on the 684, 4 miles from Leyburn
Tel: 01677 450 428
Dogs: Welcome on a lead please.
Parking: Parking on site.
Toilets: Toilets on site.

Open: 2003. 23rd March to 13th October daily 9:00am to 6:00pm.

Charges:	Adults:	£2.50
	Senior Citizens:	£2.00
	Children 5 - 16:	£0.50

Description: A large romantic garden surrounded by 18th century parkland with a superb John Carr House (not open). Fine trees, woodland walks, garden trails, rockery, extensive shrubs and roses. Set in beautiful countryside at the entrance to Wensleydale. These fine gardens feature a choice of maples planted beneath ancient yew trees, impressive daffodils in early spring and over 6,000 tulips planted annually. The reflection ponds and beckside planting are a recent development. In summer, colour and scent contribute to this romantic garden. Small plants Stall

- Events in 2003: Tulip Festival 3rd – 5th May

Leyburn
Dress Island Heritage
Theme: Craft Workshop or Shop
Address: Newsteads, High Street, Leyburn, N. Yorks.
Tel: 01969 625 005
E-mail: islandheritage@msn.com
www: www.islandheritage.co.uk
Open: Daily 10am to 5pm. (but half day Wednesday and closed Sundays, Christmas Day & Boxing Day).
Description: A wonderful unique range of eco-friendly fashions from renewable sources. Silks, cottons, Alpaca and rare breeds wool from our own farm. All without bleaches, chemicals or dyes and hand crafted to high standards. An eclectic mix of knitwear and tailored products. The fashion collection is exclusive and styles range from the traditional classic to lively fashion wear for ladies and gentlemen. Mail order catalogue available on request. See also our entry under **Masham** for **Island Heritage (Rare Breeds Wool)** (p79).

Leyburn
Elite Cinema
Theme: Cinema or Cinema Complex
Tel: 01969 624 488 **Fax:** 01969 624 651
Description: Small, friendly independent cinema. Wide range of new films. Advance booking available.

Leyburn
Middleham Castle
Theme: Castle or Castle Ruins
Directions: 2 miles south of Leyburn on the A6108.
Tel: 01969 623 899

Description: An English Heritage property. Childhood home of Richard III. Massive 12th century keep is one of the largest ever built.

Leyburn (West Burton)
Moorside Cat Pottery
Theme: Craft Workshop or Shop
Directions: 8 miles West of Leyburn off B6160 road.
Tel: 01969 663 273 or 01969 663 655
Description: Ceramic & reconstituted stone cats made in all shapes and sizes for indoors and out.

Leyburn
Tana Stained Glass
Theme: Craft Workshop or Shop
Address: Hutton Hill Farm, Constable Burton, Bedale, North Yorkshire, DL8 5RN
Tel: 07890 795050
www: www.yorkshirenet.co.uk/tanastainedglass/
Description: Design, manufacture and restoration of stained glass leaded windows. Examples can be viewed, commissions placed and items purchased.

Leyburn
Tea Pottery. The
Theme: Craft Workshop or Shop
Address: Leyburn Business Park, Leyburn, Wensleydale, North Yorkshire, DL8 5QA
Tel: 01969 623 839 **Fax:** 01969 624 079
Description: Tea, fine craftsmanship and teapots of every size, shape and style.

Leyburn
Wensleydale Longwool Sheepshop
Theme: Craft Workshop or Shop
Address: Cross Lanes Farm, Garriston, DL8 5JU
Tel: 01969 623 840
Description: Some of the most desirable hand and machine knitted garments and knitting yarns in Britain.

Leyburn
Wensleydale Railway Information Centre & Shop
Theme: Scenic Railway
Directions: On the A684 near the petrol station.
Tel: 01969 625 182
www: www.wensleydalerailway.com

Description: Selection of books, magazines, models, Thomas the Tank Engine, etc.

Leyburn (Wensley)
White Rose Candles
Theme: Craft Workshop or Shop
Directions: 2 miles West of Leyburn on the A684.
Tel: 01969 623 544 **Fax:** 01969 623 544
www: www.whiterosecandles.co.uk
Description: High quality hand made long burning candles. Aromatherapy & church candles a speciality.

Malham
Directions: 13 miles NW of Skipton on minor road off A65.
Parking: At the National Park Centre car park.
Toilets: At the National Park Centre car park.
Description: A perfectly formed corner of the Yorkshire Dales. Besides being the inspiration for Charles Kingsley's classic children's novel, The Water Babies, the area around Malham is perhaps most famous as featuring some of the finest (and most spectacular) limestone scenery in the country. Home to the glories of **Malham Cove**, **Gordale Scar**, **Malham Tarn** and limestone paving. J.M.W. Turner is just one of the many artists inspired by this dramatic landscape.

- **Malham Cove**, the 240 feet (73 metres) high limestone cliff created by the Craven Fault, was once the scene of a spectacular prehistoric waterfall. The valley above the cove is now dry, with the river having found an alternative route through an undiscovered cave system deep underground. However, at the foot of the cliff, a small stream called Malham Beck rises from a submerged cavern, which is still being explored by cave divers.
- **Gordale Scar** is a great limestone gorge some 400 feet (150 m) deep, believed by many geologists to be the remains of a huge underground cavern whose roof collapsed around the time of the last ice age. Gordale Beck cascades down the ravine in two spectacular waterfalls, one of which pours through a natural arch in the rock above. A short scramble takes visitors (at their own risk !) up the tufa deposits at the side of the first waterfall into the top section of the gorge, which leads out onto Malham Moor.
- **Malham Tarn**, a 150 acre (61 hectares) moorland lake, is set high above the village on Malham Moor. It once thundered majestically over the brink of Malham Cove, creating a waterfall higher

than Niagara. Today, despite the wildness of its location, Malham Tarn attracts many visitors to its nature reserve, where a pleasant walk leads along the shoreline to Tarn House, a remote country house which now houses a National Trust visitor centre.

At the top is a classroom geology lesson made real. Limestone paving, an expanse of exposed stone carved up like a huge jig saw, a pattern of stone blocks, "clints" and fissures between them, "grikes", a legacy of the last ice-age, 12,000 years ago.

Malham
Cove Centre
Theme: Shopping (and Visitor Centre)
Address: Wallbridge Mill, Cove Road, MALHAM, Nr Skipton, North Yorkshire, BD23 4DH
Tel: 01729 830432
Description: Walking and climbing equipment from Cave and Crag as well as a wide choice of clothing, footwear, accessories, knitwear, gifts and souvenirs.

Maltby
Roche Abbey
Theme : Abbey or Abbey Ruins
Directions: 1.5 miles South of Maltby off A634
Tel: 01709 812739
Description: Enchanting valley designed by 'Capability' Brown and the fascinating ruins of Roche Abbey founded in 1147 by the Cistercians.

Malton (Kirby Misperton)
Flamingo Land Theme Park & Zoo
Theme: Theme Park & Zoo
Directions: Kirby Misperton, off A169 Malton to Pickering Road.
Address: Flamingo Land Theme Park & Zoo, Kirby Misperton, Malton, N. Yorks, YO17 6UX
Contact:

Tel: 0870 752 8000
Fax: 01653 668 280
E-mail: info@flamingoland.co.uk
www: www.flamingoland.co.uk
Children: Hours of fun for all the family.
Disabled: Most areas accessible by wheelchair.

Dogs: Permitted - on a lead please.
Parking: FREE adjacent car and coach parking.
Toilets: Plenty throughout the Park.
Refreshments: Choose from one of many varied catering outlets.
Shop: Wide choice of gifts and souvenirs.
Facilities: Include First Aid and Lost Children.
Open: Daily from 30th March – 2nd November 2003. The Theme Park & Zoo opens daily at 10 am and closes at 5pm on weekdays and 6pm on weekends, bank holidays and during the peak season.
Charges:

Adult/child	£14.50
Family Ticket For any four people	£54.00
Senior Citizens	£7.25
Children 3 and under	FREE

Description: The best value family day out in the UK, Flamingo Land boasts more roller coasters than any theme park in the country including the triple looping coaster WALL'S MAGNUM FORCE.

2003 sees the arrival of a family ride situated in our new 10 acre themed area The Lost Kingdom now also home to hippos, rhinocerous and giraffes.

We boast six great family shows including Blomberg's Tomb of Terror, our very own haunted walk through show and the Little Monsters Music Show.

If you're hungry after all of the fun you can choose from one of many varied catering outlets.

Malton
Kirkham Priory

Theme : Priory or Priory Ruins
Directions: 5 miles SW of Malton on minor road off A64.
Tel: 01653 618 768
www: www.english-heritage.org.uk
Description: Ruins of an Augustinian priory founded c. 1125. In a peaceful valley beside the River Derwent.

Malton
Malton Museum

Theme: Museum (Archaeological)
Directions: Centre of Market Square, Malton.
Address: Old Town Hall, Market Place, Malton, N. Yorks, YO17 7LP
Tel: 01653 695 136
Open: Monday to Saturday 10.00am to 4.00pm Easter Saturday to 31st October.

Charges:
Adults: £1.50 ● Children: £1.00 ● Senior Citizens: £1.00
● Students: £1.00 ● Disabled: Standard Prices ● Family
Ticket: £4.00 (2+2) ● Groups: by arrangement
Description: Ryedale's major archaeological museum,
located in the heart of Malton's market place. The
renowned Roman collections are imaginatively
displayed. Explore the objects and evidence gathered
from local excavations, marvel at the products of the
potteries at Norton and Crambeck and admire the
evidence of the villa at Langton. Discover nearby
Orchard Fields where the ramparts of the Roman Fort
can be explored. Each year temporary exhibitions are
mounted in the upper gallery.

Malton
Scampston Hall
Theme: House or House & Garden
Address: Scampston, Malton, N. Yorks, YO17 8NG
Tel: 01944 758 224
www: www.scampston.co.uk
Description: Combining fine architecture with a wealth
of art treasures in a beautiful parkland setting. Built
about 1690 it has remained in the family ever since.

Malton
Sophie Hamilton
Theme : Craft Workshop and Shop (Pottery)
Directions: Turn off the A169 between Malton and
Pickering, follow signs to High Marishes and Thornton-
le-Dale. Deerholme pottery is the first farm on right.
Tel: 01653 668 228
www: www.sophiehamilton.co.uk
Description: Range of functional, decorative, high-fired
stoneware pots all hand decorated.

Malton
Wharram Percy
Theme: Historic Place
Directions: 6 miles SE of Malton on minor road from
B1248 half a mile South of Wharram le Street.
Tel: 0191 261 1585
Description: Ruined church & extensive earthworks of
deserted medieval village.

Masham
Black Sheep Brewery
Theme: Brewery or Brewery Visit

Directions: Masham is on the A6108 from Ripon and about 7 miles from the A1

Address: Black Sheep Brewery, Masham, North Yorkshire, HG4 4EN

Contact: Sue Dempsey

Tel: 01765 680 100

Fax: 01765 689 746

www: www.visitor.centre@blacksheep.co.uk

Disabled: The Bistro Baa....r and Shop are all wheelchair friendly. However, due to the number of stairs, the full brewery tour is inaccessible to wheelchairs. A shortened tour can be arranged with prior notice.

Dogs: Guide dogs only.

Parking: Coach and car parking on site.

Facilities: Toilets, refreshments and a shop on site

Open:

The **Visitor Centre** is open daily.

- Wednesday to Saturday: 10:00am to 11:00pm **throughout the year** and
- Sunday, Monday & Tuesday: 10:00 am. to 5:30pm **Except** January & February: 10:00 am. to **4:30pm**

Black Sheep Brewery Tour Times

- March to December: 11:00, 12:30, 2:00, 3:00 & 4:00
- January & February: 11:30, 12:30; 2:00 & 3:00

Charges: There are no admission charges to the visitor centre, the bistro and the shop. Charges do apply to shepherded tours.

Awards: Brewer of the Year - 2001

Description:

A POTTED HISTORY

The Black Sheep Brewery was established in the early 90s and its first brews were sampled in 1992, but in one sense you wouldn't be wrong about the 'timeless' feel of the brewery. As the fifth generation of Masham's famous brewing family, Paul Theakston is aware that Black Sheep has a lot to live up to. The vessels, plant and methods employed here are from a bygone era. The building itself is part of the former Lightfoot Brewery, which Paul's grandfather took over in 1919.

Paul left his former family firm T & R Theakston in 1989 after a takeover by Scottish and Newcastle Breweries. It would almost seem as if fate has a conscience because as if to make amends the old maltings which had previously been part of Lightfoot's became available.

SHEPHERDED TOURS

You'll experience the Black Sheep brewing process, from the aroma and taste of English hops, malted barley and pure, clean Dales water to the end product: a glass of one of our traditionally brewed Black Sheep beers. You'll see our traditional brewhouse and the fermenting room complete with our own Yorkshire Square fermenting vessels. The 'shepherded' brewery tour takes approximately one hour.

BAR AND BISTRO

The spacious split-level bistro has a warm welcoming atmosphere. It is open through the day for snacks, lunches, teas, and coffees, and in the evening for delicious 'a la carte' meals. It's unusual surroundings, interesting local menu and friendly staff make the bistro a 'ewenique' eating experience. Special diets can be catered for with prior notice.

BLACK SHEEP SHOP

The Black Sheep Shop is full of surprises, with gifts for all occasions from Black Sheep clothing to cuddly sheep to Black Sheep Ale and Riggwelter gift packs. With over 1,000 different items there is something for everyone. They also have a mail-order catalogue that includes their best selling items and they offer their own 'ewenique' hamper service.

THE BREWHOUSE

The brewhouse was installed in the summer of 1992, and sits in what was the kiln of a former rnaltings. It is laid out in the traditional tower fashion, whereby rnashtun, copper and hop back are positioned one above the other, with gravity taking the brew down through the process. Fermentation takes place in Yorkshire Squares. Some of the vessels are made of slate and are over 80 years old. Traditional varieties of both rnalting barley and hops, brewed according to time honoured methods, go to creating Black Sheep beers.

BLACK SHEEP ALES

The Black Sheep Brewery currently produces five ales. Black Sheep Best Bitter, a full bodied session beer, ABV 3.8%. Black Sheep Ale, distinctly stronger and darker than the Best Bitter is a fine beer with a truly old fashioned flavour, ABV 4.4%. Yorkshire Square Ale, surprisingly pale and easy drinking for a strong ale, ABV 5.0%. Riggwelter, a deep chestnut brown beer with a near white head, ABV 5.9% and Monty Python's Holy Grail Ale, ABV 4.7%, specially commissioned to commemorate the 30th anniversary of Monty Python, which has a distinctive flavour with plenty of fruity hops and a dry and refreshing bitterness.

Riggwelter, Yorkshire Square Ale, Monty Python's Holy Grail Ale and Black Sheep Ale are available in bottles. Black Sheep Ale is the number 4 premium bottled beer in the country.

Masham
Island Heritage (Rare Breeds Wool)

Theme: Craft Workshop or Shop
Directions: Leave Masham on the A6108 towards Middleham then left to Fearby & Healey.
Address: Pott Hall Farm, Leighton Reservoir, Healey, Masham, N. Yorks, HG4 4LT
Tel: 01765 689 651
E-mail: islandheritage@msn.com
www: www.islandheritage@hotmail.co.uk
Open: 1st April to 31st October 10am to 6pm. Daily (but closed Tuesdays) • 1st November to 31st March 11am to 4pm. Daily (but closed Tuesdays, Christmas Day & Boxing Day).
Description: A working Dales farm producing an eclectic mix of knitwear and tailored products from rare breeds of sheep. The fashion collection is exclusive and styles range from the traditional classic to lively fashion wear for ladies and gentlemen. Mail order catalogue available on request.

See our entry under **Leyburn** for **Dress Island Heritage** (p71).

Masham
Jervaulx Abbey
Theme: Abbey or Abbey Ruins

Directions: Mid-way between Masham and Leyburn on the A6108.
Tel: 01677 460 226 & 01677 460 391 (Tea Rooom)
Disabled: Limited access in Abbey, toilets available at Tea Room.
Parking: Parking on site for Tea Room. 110 metre walk to Abbey (from car park) through parkland.
Toilets: At Tea Room.
Refreshments: Tea Room opens in March till 1st November. Seating for 60 people.
Open: Open all year, daily, dawn-dusk.
Charges: £2.00 (Adults) £1.50 (Children)
Description:
- Privately owned site with the remains of a splendid Cistercian Abbey.
- Guided tours available by appointment.
- Tea Room opens in March till 1st November. Seating for 60 people.
- Abbey is open all year round.

Masham
Swinton Park

Theme: Hotel and Restaurant
Directions: Take the B6267 exit off the A1 and follow signs to Masham. Take the road through the town centre. Turn right at Swinton Terrace, after 1 mile the gate house is on the right.
Tel: 01765 680 900
E-mail: enquiries@swintonpark.com
www: www.swintonpark.com

Children: Welcome. Baby changing facilities available.
Disabled: Facilities available.
Dogs: Welcome if well behaved - in bedrooms but not public areas.
Parking: Parking on site
Toilets: Toilets on site
Refreshments: Refreshments on site
Open: All year
Description: Splendidly restored 30 bedroom castle hotel with 200 acres of gardens, lakes and parkland and Samuel's fine dining restaurant. Fully open for morning coffee, lunch, bar snacks, dinner & afternoon teas.

Masham
Uredale Glass

Theme: Craft Workshop and Shop
Directions: On the A6108, 10 miles from Ripon or the B6267, 10 minutes from the A1. Just off the large market square, walk through the King's Head archway and we are about 50 metres behind the hotel.
Tel: 01765 689 780
E-mail: info@uredale.co.uk
www: www.uredale.co.uk

Facilities: Children & disabled are welcome as are dogs at owner's risk. Parking, toilets and refreshments are available in the town square.
Admission: Free
Open:
- Glass making Monday to Friday (5 days a week)
- Summer: Daily from Easter to end of October 10:00am to 5:00pm.
- Winter: Monday to Friday 10:00am to 4:30pm.
- January: Please check opening hours.

Description: A wide range of highly collectable glass from one-off pieces for collectors to small gifts, lighting and stemware. Each piece is individually stamped.

Middleham (Leyburn)
Forbidden Corner. The

Theme: Visitor Attraction
Directions: Follow signs for Middleham. Take the Coverdale road across the moor and past Coverharn church. Turn right opposite the cottages, through the big iron gates and carry on up through the park. The entrance is under the clocktower.
Address: Tupgill Park Estate, Coverham, Middleham, Leyburn, N. Yorkshire, DL8 4TJ
Contact: John or Wendy Reeves.
Tel: 01969 640 638 or 01969 640 687
Fax: 01969 640 687

www: www.yorkshirenet.co.uk/theforbiddencorner

Children: Suitable for children of all ages.

Disabled: Some parts of the garden are disabled accessible.

Dogs: Sorry, no dogs in the garden.

Parking: Available on site.

Toilets: Available on site.

Refreshments: Available on site.

Shop: Gift and souvenir shop on site.

Open:

- Daily from the 1st April – 31st October and then Sundays until Christmas
- Monday to Saturday 12 - 6pm
- Sundays & Bank Holidays 10am - 6pm (or dusk if earlier)
- Admission is only by booking. Call John or Wendy Reeves on 01969 640 638 or 01969 640 687 to reserve your ticket. Or call into Leyburn Tourist Information Centre on the day of your visit. **Please note** T-I-C tickets are limited and sold on a first come first served basis.

Charges: Adults: £6 • OAP's: £5 • Children: £4 • Family Ticket (2 adults + 2 children): £19.00

Awards: Voted the best European folly of the 20th Century (The Folly Fellowship). Voted best children's attraction in Yorkshire (calendar) Yorkshire TV.

Description: The Forbidden Corner is a delightful four acres (1.6 hectares) walled garden folly. Lose yourself in the underground labyrinth of chambers and passages which are the grotto. Discover intrigue and humour throughout the wood where follies abound. There are decisions to make and tricks to avoid. A day out with a difference which will challenge and delight all ages.

Middlesbrough

Captain Cook's Birthplace Museum

Theme: Museum

Directions: Turn off the A19 onto the A174, then North on the A172, from where the Museum is sign posted.

Tel: 01642 311 211

www: www.middlesbrough.gov.uk

Description: Looks at the life and voyages of the 18th century explorer. Stands close to Cook's birthplace. See also the **Captain Cook Memorial Museum** at Whitby (p120), and the **Captain Cook Schoolroom Museum** at Great Ayton (p43).

Muker (near Richmond)
Swaledale Woollens

Theme: Craft Workshop or Shop
Directions: 20 miles from Richmond, 10 from Reeth on the B6270 or 6 from Hawes across the Buttertubs Pass.
Tel/Fax: 01748 886 251
E-mail: woollens@swaledale.net
www: www.swaledalewoollens.co.uk
Description: The lovely Dales village of Muker has been our home for over 30 years. Visitors come from all corners of the world to buy from our unique range of quality garments in beautiful harmonious country colours, all hand made by a dedicated team of skilled knitters. Worldwide mail order service available. Please ask for our latest brochure.

Northallerton
Battle of The Standard

Theme: Battle. Site of
Description: Two miles north of Northallerton, near the Darlington road. A stone obelisk marks the site. On the 22nd August 1138 the Scots, under King David were heavily defeated by the barons of the North of England.

Northallerton
Bettys Café Tea Rooms

Theme: Refreshments
Address: 188 High Street, Northallerton
Tel: 01609 775154
Description: Also at Harrogate, Ilkley and York. For a fuller description see our entry under "**York**" (p123).

Northallerton (Osmotherley)
Mount Grace Priory

Theme: Priory or Priory Ruins
Directions: Just N of the Osmotherley exit off the A19.
Tel: 01609 883 494
Description: An English Heritage property. The Carthusian Order reverted to the ancient and Eastern pattern of solitary lives with the monks living like hermits, in isolation, each in his own cell, to which his meals were brought.

Northallerton (Osmotherley)
Sheepwash Picnic spot

Theme: Scenic Area
Description: North of the village. The ancient Drovers' Road descends from the moors here on route for Yarm and River Tees.

Pateley Bridge (Lofthouse)
How Stean Gorge

Theme: Cave or Caves (Limestone Gorge & Tom Taylor's Cave & Restaurant)
Directions: 7 miles NW of Pately Bridge on minor road.
Address: Lofthouse, Harrogate, North Yorks, HG3 5SF
Tel: 01423 755 666
Disabled: Access to Restaurant but not Gorge or Cave.
Facilities: Parking, toilets, Gift Shop & Restaurant serving English food. Children welcome.
Open: All year 10:00am - 6:00pm. ● Restaurant closed Mondays and Tuesdays in January and February
● Evening meals served April to end of September.
Charges: Admission charge to Gorge & Cave.
Description: Spectacular limestone gorge set in Nidderdale's lush green pastures.

Pateley Bridge
Nidderdale Museum

Theme: Museum

Directions: On the B-6165 14 miles West of Harrogate.
Address: King Street, Pateley Bridge, Harrogate, N. Yorks, HG3 5LE(opposite the church)
Tel: 01423 711 225
www: www.harrogate.gov.uk/museums
Disabled: Limited disabled access, toilet, chair lift, wheelchair available.
Parking: FREE at Museum (restricted).
Open: Easter to November: daily 1:30 to 4:30pm ● August: daily 11:00am to 4:30pm ● November to Easter: Weekends only 1:30 to 4:30pm
Charges: Adult: £2.00 ● Concessions: £1 ● Child: £1.00 (School age).
Awards: National Heritage Museum of the year award.
Description: Has featured on television programmes. Fascinating collection of exhibits displayed in the original Victorian workhouse, beautifully illustrating the life and history of Dales folk. An imaginative series of

displays includes a complete Cobbler's Shop, General Store, Victorian Parlour, Kitchen & Schoolroom, Chemist's, Haberdasher's, Joiners Shop and new displays on agriculture, transport and industries in 12 rooms.

Pickering
Beck Isle Museum of Rural Life
Theme: Museum (Rural Life)
Address: Bridge Street, Pickering, N. Yorks
Tel: 01751 473 653
Description: Contains a collection of bygones relating largely to the rural crafts and living style of Ryedale.

Pickering (Thornton-le-Dale)
Bridestones Moor
Theme: Land or Seascape
Directions: 3$^1/_2$ miles along Dalby Forest Drive.
Description: Famous for peculiar shaped formations.

Pickering
Cropton Brewery
Theme: Brewery or Brewery Visit
Directions: New Inn car park, Cropton Village.
Tel: 01751 417 330
www: www.croptonbrewery.co.uk
Description: Award winning beers. Taste the different malts, smell the aromatic hop flowers, savour a sample.

Pickering (Thornton-le-Dale)
Dalby Forest
Theme: Scenic Drive (and woodland)
Directions: 2 miles north of Thornton-le-Dale on Whitby Road.
Address: Forest Enterprise, Outgang Road, Pickering, N. Yorks, YO18 7EL.
Tel: 01751 472 771. Visitor Centre 01751 460 295
Fax: 01751 474 503
E-mail: n.yorks.moors.fdo@forestry.gsi.gov.uk
www: www.forestry.gov.uk/dalbyforest
Children: Play furniture.
Disabled: Toilets and Visitor Centre are wheelchair friendly. All ability trails.
Dogs: Welcome. Must be kept under control – please.
Parking: Unlimited parking available on site.
Toilets: Three toilet blocks on site.
Refreshments: Available near Visitor Centre.
Shop: Selection of gifts, souvenirs and information.
Facilities: Include an informative Visitor Centre.
Open: Daily all year round, dawn to dusk'

Charges: £4.00 per car; April to October.
£1.50 per car, other times.
Description: Dalby Forest offers over 8,000 acres of woodland to explore and enjoy ● The 9 mile drive gives access to play areas for the kids, barbeques for the family and plenty of waymarked trails for all abilities ● For those who like to relax, there's always a quiet corner to watch the wildlife and take in the fresh air and scenery.

Pickering
North Yorkshire Moors Railway
Theme: Scenic Railway

Directions: Pickering town centre.
Address: North Yorkshire Moors Railway, Pickering Station, North Yorkshire, YO18 7AJ
Tel: 01751 472 508
Fax: 01751 476 970
E-mail: admin@nympickering.fsnet.co.uk
www: www.northyorkshire moors railway.com
Disabled: Access available
Dogs: Yes
Parking: Yes
Toilets: Yes
Refreshments: Pickering, Goathland and Grosmont, buffet trolleys on most trains.
Shop: Pickering, Goathland and Grosmont.
Open: Daily 29th March to 2nd November
Charges: *All day, all line, return tickets* ● Adult £12.00 ● Child £6.00 ● Over 60 £10.00. ● *Single journey & family tickets also available.*
Events: Special events held throughout the year.
Description: Pickering: Lovely market town with medieval castle and church, Beck Isle Museum, Pickering Trout Lake, speciality shops and Monday street market. ● **Levisham**: gateway to Newton Dale, dramatic glacial valley and walkers' paradise. ●
Newton Dale Halt: The heart of beautiful Newton Dale and starting point for three waymarked woodland walks. Tell the Guard if you wish to alight here. ● **Grosmont**: The NYMR's operational headquarters and engine sheds where locos can be viewed under restoration or preparing for the next journey. At Grosmont you can connect with National Railways services to Whitby. ● **Goathland**: Now famous as Heartbeat's 'Aidensfield'. Explore the village or walk the Historical Rail Trail to Grosmont along the trackbed of Stephenson's original route.

Pickering
Pickering Castle
Theme: Castle or Castle Ruins
Directions: East of the town centre on Castle Road
Tel: 01751 474 989
Description: 12th century castle and royal hunting lodge.

Pickering
Pickering Castle Cinema
Theme: Cinema or Cinema Complex
Directions: Follow signs for the Castle.
Address: 10 - 11, Burgate, Pickering, YO18 7AU
Tel: 01751 472622 **Fax:** 01751 472622
Children: Indoor play centre, ballpool, slides, bouncy castle etc.
Disabled: Access through back fire exit. Please ask.
Dogs: Sorry! No dogs.
Refreshments: Sandwiches, hot drinks, snacks etc.
Facilities: Include toilets and shop.
Open: Evening Shows: 7.30pm daily ● Matinees: 2pm weekends and school holidays.
Charges: Adults: £3.70 ● Under 16s & OAPs £2.70 ● Family Tickets (2 Adults + 2 Children): £10.00

Pickering
Pickering Traction Engine Rally
Theme: Rally
Directions: Pickering Showfield A169 Malton Road
Tel: 01751 473 780
www: www.theeventsoffice.co.uk
Open: July 31st, August 1st, 2nd and 3rd.
Description: Showmans Engines, Fairground Organs, Historic Cars and Vintage Commercial Vehicles.

Pickering
Pickering Trout Lake & Moorland Trout Farm
Theme: Fishing
Directions: Next to North Yorkshire Moors Railway
Tel: Pickering Trout Lake 01751 474 219 ● Moorland Trout Farm 01751 473 101
Description: Pickering Trout Lake. Float fishing for all the family and fly fishing for the more experienced. Lake well stocked with 'good eating' rainbow trout. **Moorland Trout Farm.** Walk round and feed the fish. Oak smoked and fresh trout available.

Pocklington
Burnby Hall Gardens and Museum

Theme: Garden or Gardens

Directions: Just off the A1079 York to Hull road.

Address: Stewart's Burnby Hall Gardens and Museum Trust, The Balk, Pocklington, York, YO42 2QF

Contact: Resident Warden

Tel: 01759 302 068

E-mail: info@burnbyhallgardens.co.uk

www: www.burnbyhallgardens.co.uk

Children: Play area designed to meet the needs of disabled and able-bodied children and has proved hugely popular.

Disabled: Easily accessible to wheelchairs, with special viewing platforms to allow disabled to feed the fish and see the lilies at close quarters in safety. There are ramps into the Tearooms.

Dogs: With the exception of guide dogs for the blind and the hard of hearing dogs are not admitted to the Gardens.

Parking: Car park adjacent to entrance.

Toilets: Two special toilets for the disabled together with mother and baby changing facilities.

Refreshments: Café and tearooms.

Shop: Wide variety of mementoes and souvenirs to suit all ages and pockets. Wide variety of reasonably priced seasonal plants, shrubs and ornamental stoneware.

Open: Daily 10.00am to 6.00pm. March 29th 2003 to September 28th, 2003. Last admittance is at 5.00pm.

Charges: Adults £2.70 ● Senior Citizens £2.20 ● Children (5–15 inclusive) £1.20 ● Under-five **FREE** ● Parties of 20 or over. £1.75

Awards: Age Concern award winners.

Events: Regular Sunday afternoon band concerts.

Description: What is claimed to be Europe's finest display of waterlilies. ● Whether you are an enthusiast, or simply want to see beautiful water lilies in a natural setting, Burnby Hall Gardens is the place to be. ● The water lilies have been designated a 'National Collection' and more varieties can be seen here, in their natural habitat, than anywhere else in Europe. ● We should not forget the extensive range of ornamental trees, plants, shrubs, flowers, and the numerous fish and birds which thrive in our special habitat. ● Huge collection of Koi Carp and other species of fish enjoy being fed by our visitors. Special fish food is on sale at the entrance. ●

Within the grounds, you will find The Museum, which offers a fascinating glimpse into the life of Major Stewart, our founder and benefactor, who toured the world in the early part of the 20th century.

Pontefract
Pontefract Castle

Theme: Castle or Castle Ruins
Description: Became a royal castle in 1399. During the Civil War it was held by the King's supporters but after 1649, it was largely demolished. The remains of the castle and the underground magazine chamber are open to visitors.

Pontefract
Pontefract Races

Theme: Horse Racing
Directions: The entrance is only half a mile from junction 32 of the M62. The M62 passes the northern side of the track and links with the A1, M1 and M18 within 10 miles of the Course
Address: Pontefract Park Race Co. Ltd. 33 Ropergate, Pontefract, West Yorkshire, WF8 1LE. (Administration)
Contact: J. N. Gundill, Esq.
Tel: 01977 703224
Fax: 01977 600577
E-mail: info@pontefract-races.co.uk
www: www.pontefract-races.co.uk/
Children: Accompanied under 16s are FREE
Disabled: Welcome. Lift access in Club.
Dogs: Not permitted.
Parking: Extensive and FREE.
Facilities: Stands with refreshments & toilets throughout course.
Open: ● April; 8th, 14th, 30th ● May: 23rd (Evening)
● June: 1st (Sunday), 9th (Evening), 22nd (Sunday), 30th
● July: 8th, 18th (Evening) ● August: 6th, 17th (Sunday)
● September: 18th, 25th ● October: 6th, 20th ●
Charges: £3 to £15 dependent on enclosure. Please 'phone for group discounts.
Description: Pontefract stages Britain's longest handicap on the Flat, The Tote Marathon Handicap and is the longest continuous flat course in Europe. Every meeting stages entertaining and competitive racing.

Redcar
Redcar Races

Theme: Horse Racing
Directions: Situated in the town, sign posted from the A1085 and A174 from Teesside, with entrances on Redcar Lane and West Dyke Road. Redcar Central train station is only a few minutes' walk from the course.
Address: Redcar Racecourse Ltd., The Racecourse, Redcar, Cleveland, TS10 2BY.
Tel: 01642 484068
Fax: 01642 488272
E-mail: info@redcarracing.co.uk
www: www.redcarracing.co.uk/
Open: 18 fixtures between May and November. Please ring for details or visit our website.
Charges:
● **Members**: £15 ● **Tattersalls**: £10; (OAP) £5 ●
Course £3.50; (OAP) £2.
● **Concessions for pre-booked parties** of 12+:
Members: £11; *Tattersalls*: £5.50; *Course*: £2.50. Plus one free ticket for every 20 purchased.
Description: Yorkshire's 'Seaside Racecourse'. There has been racing on the present site at Redcar on the Cleveland coast since 1872.

Reeth
Clockworks

Theme: Craft Workshop or Shop
Address: Silver Street, Reeth, Richmond, DL11 6SP
Tel: 01748 884 088
Description: Clocks and barometers made to order, repaired and restored. Showroom display.

Reeth
Marrick Priory

Theme: Priory or Priory Ruins
Directions: Seven miles west-southwest of Richmond
Description: Former Benedictine nunnery, 1155. Now run as Marrick Priory Centre for Outdoor Education.

Reeth
Philip Bastow, Cabinet Maker

Theme: Craft Workshop or Shop
Directions: Reeth Dales Centre, Silver Street, Reeth.
Tel: 01748 884 555
Description: Philip Bastow specialises in the design and manufacture of individual furniture commissions.

Reeth
Pots 'n' Presents
Theme: Craft Workshop or Shop
Address: Anvil Square, Reeth, Richmond, DL11 6TE
Tel: 01748 884 687
Description: Traditional hand thrown pottery, glazed in a variety of colours synonymous with the Dales.

Reeth
Shades of Heather Rugs

Theme: Craft Workshop
Speciality: Rug making
Directions: The Garden Studio, Greencroft, Reeth
Tel: 01748 884 435
E-mail: rugmaker@clara.net
www: rugmaker.co.uk
Open: Visitors are strictly by appointment only please. Ring or send for details.
Description: Visit Heather's garden studio to learn or improve traditional rug making skills - hooking, prodding and dyeing wools. One day or residential workshops. Full range of equipment for sale including a teaching video on how to make rag rugs. All hooks are beautifully hand crafted out of hardwoods, all sizes. Mail order facility. Send for details.

Reeth
Stef's Models
Theme: Craft Workshop, or shop (Animal Models)
Directions: Reeth Dales Centre, Silver Street, Reeth.
Tel: 01748 884 498
Description: See the production process from design through mould making, casting and hand painting.

Reeth
Swaledale Folk Museum

Theme: Museum
Directions: Reeth Green, Reeth
Tel: 01748 884 373
www:
www.yorkshirenet.co.uk/visinfo/swlfolkm/index.html
Children: Welcome
Disabled: Welcome
Dogs: Welcome
Parking: On Reeth Green
Toilets: On Reeth Green
Refreshments: On Reeth Green
Open: Good Friday to Oct 31st. Every day 10:30am to 5:00pm.
Charges: Adults £2; Children 50p
Description: Visit the unique Folk Museum and see the way of life of the past.

Displays include leadmining, stone walling, sheep and cattle farming, handknitting, joiner, tinsmith, homemaking, Proddy rugs, patchwork plus much more.

Richmond
Aske Hall

Theme: House or House & Garden
Address: Aske Hall, Richmond, N. Yorks, DL10 5HJ
Tel: 01748 822 000
Description: A Georgian gem, with chapel, folias, terraced garden and lake in Capability Brown parkland. Phone to check opening days, times & charges.

Richmond
Easby Abbey

Theme: Abbey or Abbey Ruins
Directions: 1 mile South East of Richmond off B6271.
Tel: 0191 269 1214
Description: An English Heritage property. 12th century Abbey of the Premonstatensian Order ruins.

Richmond
Georgian Theatre Royal and Museum

Theme: Theatre or Playhouse
Address: Victoria Road off Friars Wynd, Richmond, North Yorkshire, DL10 4DW
Contact: Jayne Duncan
Tel: 01748 823 710
www: georgiantheatre.com

Disabled: Partial disabled access.
Toilets: Toilets on site
Facilities: Theatre ● Museum • Coffee shop
Open: Under refurbishment ● Due to open June 2003
Charges: Telephone to check.
Events: Brochure available on request.
Description: Built in 1788, oldest working theatre in its original form in Europe. Closed in 1848, it was an auction room, corn chandlers shop, furniture warehouse and salvage depot before being restored and reopened in 1962. The original pit, boxes and gallery remain.

Richmond
Green Howards Museum

Theme: Museum
Tel: 01748 822 133
www: www.greenhowards.org.uk
Children: Free
Disabled: Stannah lifts to all galleries.
Dogs: Not allowed
Parking: In market square
Toilets: In square
Refreshments: Next door café
Open: April to October: Monday to Saturday 9:30am to 4:30pm. Closed Sunday - except mid May to September open 2:00pm to 4:30pm
November to March: Monday to Friday 10:00am to 4:00pm but closed December and January
Charges: Adults: £2.50; Concessions: £2.00; Children: FREE.
Description: One of the finest military Museums in England.
- Winner of the White Rose Award for Tourism 1998.
- The 315 year history of this famous Yorkshire Regiment.
- Interactive videos WW I and WW II and CD ROM.
- Audio Guide to uniforms, weapons, medals and war relics.
- Also, Richmond Town's antique silver.

Richmond
Kiplin Hall
Theme: House or House & Garden

Directions: Off the B6271 between Scorton and Northallerton, 5 miles East of the A1.
Tel: 01748 818 178
Description: Jacobean country house built in 1620. Grade I listed Hall is filled with fine paintings & furniture

Richmond (Gunnerside)
Old Working Smithy
Theme: Museum
Address: Gunnerside, Richmond, DL11 6LE
Tel: 01748 886 577
Description: View a collection of blacksmithing, leadmining and farming artefacts and photographs.

Richmond
Richmond Castle
Theme: Castle or Castle Ruins
Directions: In Richmond town centre.
Tel: 01748 822 493
Description: An English Heritage property. The oldest castle in Great Britain. Built by William the Conqueror as a mighty fortress and palatial residence.

Richmond
Richmondshire Museum

THE JAMES HERRIOT VET'S SURGERY SET
Theme: Museum.
Speciality: Local history.
Directions: In Ryders Wynd, Richmond.
Tel: 01748 825 611
www: communigate.co.uk/ne/richmondshiremuseum
Facilities: Children and disabled welcome. Toilets and shop on site.
Open: Daily. April to October: 10:30am to 4:30pm - last admission 4:00pm.
Charges: Adults: £1.50; OAPs and children: £1.00; Family Ticket: £4.00.
Description: The history of Richmond and its people, including James Herriot set. Displays about lead mining, transport, domestic bygones. Chemist's shop. Dales Post Office.

Ripley
Ripley Castle

Theme: House or House & Garden
Directions: 3 miles North of Harrogate on the A61.
Tel: 01423 770 152
www: www.ripleycastle.co.uk
Description: Where Trooper Jane Ingilby, daughter of the house and a staunch royalist, held Oliver Cromwell at gunpoint in the castle's Library. Walled gardens.

Ripon
Christ the Consoler's Church

Theme: Church or Church Ruins
Directions: Newby Hall Grounds, 4-Miles SEof Ripon.
www: www.visitchurches.org.uk
Description: Built in 1871-76 as an extravagant memorial to a young man, Frederick Vyner, murdered by brigands while travelling in Greece. Everything is on a magnificent scale; the effect is overwhelming.

Ripon
Courthouse Museum

Theme: Museum
Directions: Courthouse Museum is in Minster Road.
Tel: 01765 690799
Description: Ripon's historic courtroom still retains much of its original character.

Ripon
Fountains Abbey & Studley Royal Water Garden

Theme: Abbey or Abbey Ruins
Directions: 4 miles West of Ripon off the B6265 road.
Tel: 01765 608 888
Description: A National Trust property. Awarded World Heritage status in 1987. Perhaps the finest monastic ruin in Europe, dating back to 1132. The Water Garden is one of the most spectacular in England.

Ripon
Lightwater Country Shopping Village

Theme: Shopping Outlet
Directions: Take the A6108, or signed from the A1 and A61. Just 5 minutes from A1, 3 miles north of Ripon.
Address: North Stainley, Ripon, N. Yorks, HG4 3HT
Contact: Marketing Department.
Tel: 0870 458 0040

Fax: 01765 635 359
E-mail: leisure@lightwatervalley.co.uk
www: www.lightwatervalley.net
Children: Play area – FREE.
Disabled: Facilities for wheelchair users.
Dogs: Not admitted except guide dogs.
Parking: FREE.
Toilets: Various locations.
Refreshments: Granary Coffee Shop and Restaurant.
Shop: 30,000 sq ft of shopping selling clothes, gifts, plants, home furnishings and much more.
Facilities: Include Bird of Prey Centre (small charge).
Open: Open all year round from 10am.
Charges: Free entrance and parking.
Description: Set in the country, Lightwater Shopping Village offers a tranquil shopping experience with entertainment for the kids.

Ripon

Lightwater Valley Theme Park

Theme: Theme Park
Directions: Take the A6108, or signed from the A1 and A61. Just 5 minutes from A1, 3 miles north of Ripon.
Address: North Stainley, Ripon, N. Yorks, HG4 3HT
Contact: Marketing Department.
Tel: 0870 458 0060
Fax: 01765 635 539
E-mail: leisure@lightwatervalley.co.uk
www: www.lightwatervalley.net
Children: Facilities available for children of all ages.
Disabled: Facilities available for disabled visitors.
Dogs: Not admitted except Guide Dogs.
Parking: FREE.
Toilets: Various locations around the park.
Refreshments: Pub in the wood serving alcoholic beverages and snacks. Conservatory and Riviera Food Court serving fast food. Various snackbars also on site. Picnic site. Granary restaurant serving full range of hot food.
Shop: Various locations around the park.
Open: Easter to October. Daily during June, July and August. Call to check dates and times.
Charges: Admission charges apply.
Events: Check with venue for a list of special events.
Description: Set in 175 acres of parkland, featuring a number of white-knuckle rides; The Ultimate Rollercoaster, Caterpillar Coaster and Grizzly Bear, Go-Karting, Falls of Terror, leisurely train/boat rides, soft play area, Carousel Putting, a variety of entertainment for all the family, restaurant, café, snackbars and picnic areas. A village of factory outlet shops selling stylish fashions, great gift ideas and inspired home furnishings.

Ripon
Markenfield Hall
Theme: House & Moated Garden

Directions: 3 miles South of Ripon off A-61.
Address: Markenfield Hall, Ripon, N. Yorks, HG4 3AD
Contact: The Administrator.
Tel: 01765 603 411 **Fax:** 01765 607 195
www: www.markenfield.com
Children: Welcome
Disabled: Difficult wheelchair access.
Dogs: On a lead only please and not in the house.
Parking: For 35 next to Gatehouse.
Toilets: Available on site.
Facilities: Guidebooks and postcards available.
Licensed for civil marriages with Service of Blessing in medieval chapel if required.
Open:
Daily 2pm-5pm
Sunday 4th May to Sunday 18th May
Sunday 15th June to Sunday 29th June
Open at other times to groups by appointment with a guided tour.
Charges: Admission
Adult £3
Children and concessions £2.
Events: Catholic and Anglican services (some choral) held regularly in the Chapel – ask for Schedule of services
Description: • A completely moated and fortified Manor House built in 1310 • Starting point of the Rising of the North in 1569 • "This wonderfully little-altered building is the most complete surviving example of the medium-sized fourteenth century house in England" - J R Robinson, The Architecture of Northern England. • "Surely one of the most romantic houses left in England" - D B Camm, Forgotten Shrines.

Ripon
Newby Hall and Gardens
Theme: House & Garden
Directions: Off B6265 Ripon to Boroughbridge road.
Tel: 01423 322 583
www: www.newbyhall.com
Description: One of England's renowned Adam houses. Superb contents. Award-winning gardens. Children's Adventure Garden. Miniature Railway.

Ripon
Norton Conyers

Theme: House & Garden
Directions: From Ripon take A61 for Thirsk, left at top of hill for Wath/Norton Conyers. From A1 turn off at Baldersby flyover onto A61 to Ripon, turn right at turning marked "Melmerby".
Tel: 01765 640 333
E-mail: norton.conyers@ripon.org
Disabled: Ramp at entrance.
Dogs: Guide dogs only in house. Allowed in garden if on lead.
Parking: Parking on site.
Toilets: Toilets in house (for disabled) and garden.
Refreshments: For booked parties and at garden charity openings.
Open: 2003:
Dates: **House & Garden**
- Easter Sunday and Monday
- Bank Holiday Sundays and Mondays
- Sundays 11th May to 7th September
- Daily 7th July to 12th July
- The Garden is also open on Thursdays throughout the year from 10:00 am to 4:00 pm (please check beforehand).

Times:
- **House**   2:00 pm to 5:00 pm
- **Garden**   12:00 am to 5:00 pm
  Last Admissions 4:40 pm

Charges:
- **House**:   Adults; £4.00, OAPs £3.00
  Children; (aged 10 -16) £3.00
  Reduced rate for 2 or more children
  Booked parties by arrangement.

- **Garden**: Admission is free: donations are welcome. A charge is made when the garden is open for charity.

Description: This late medieval house with Stuart and Georgian additions has belonged to the Grahams since 1624. The pictures and furniture reflect 378 years of occupation by the same family. Charles I and James II visited it as did Charlotte Brontë; a family legend of a mad woman who had been confined in the attics is said to have given her the idea for the mad Mrs. Rochester in "Jane Eyre", while the house is an original of Mr. Rochester's Thornfield Hall.

Family wedding dresses and other costumes are on display.

Please note that ladies are requested not to wear stiletto-heeled shoes. Photography of the interior is not allowed except by the owner's written permission.

The 18th century walled garden, with its herbaceous borders, small pond and Orangery, is about 100 metres from the house. Unusual hardy plants are for sale as is pick-your-own fruit in season - intending pickers are advised to check beforehand.

Ripon
Prison & Police Museum
Theme: Museum
Directions: St. Marygate, Ripon.
Tel: 01765 690 799
Description: Illustrates the harsh conditions of prison life as 200 years of policing are displayed.

Ripon
Ripon Canal & Marina
Theme: Canal or Inland Waterway
Directions: Follow B6265 off the A1. Turn left after the entrance to Ripon Racecourse.
Address: British Waterways, North Yorkshire Navigations, 5 Bramley's Barn, The Menagerie, Skipwith Road, Escrick, York YO19 6ET
Contact: Jonathen Slater
Tel: 01904 728229
Fax: 01904 728860
E-mail: jonathen.slater@britishwaterways.co.uk
www: www.britishwaterways.co.uk
Children: Welcome, educational visits encouraged
Disabled: Welcome, access for all facilities
Dogs: Welcome
Parking: On site
Toilets: Boaters and pre-booked groups only

Refreshments: Drinks machine in the Smeaton Centre
Open: Smeaton Centre open 10 am – 4 pm daily
Charges: Free entry into Smeaton Centre. Moorings available, please contact the office at Escrick
Awards: British Waterways' 2001 and 2002 regional award for best maintained canal length and 1999 national award for best maintained canal length
Description: Ripon Marina offers moorings for 80 craft with electricity, water, lighting and sanitary facilities on site. Craft can cruise the system via the Rivers Ouse and Ure, the Selby Canal or venture further afield, to the Humber estuary, Hull Marina, or the North Sea.

The Smeaton Information Centre at the Marina was opened in 2002. This new facility is an ideal place for visitors to the area and the community of Ripon to sit and read about the canal history and environment.

Enjoy the new 3-mile access for all circular walk around the canal and view the boats and adjacent wetlands area, local heritage and wildlife.

Ripon
Ripon Cathedral
Theme: Cathedral or Cathedral Ruins
Directions: Just a short walk from the City Centre.
Tel: 01765 603 462 or 01765 602 072
www: www.riponcathedral.org.uk
Description: Founded in the 7th century, this historic Cathedral of the Dales is among the finest in Britain. St. Wilfrid's crypt (AD 672) is one of the oldest in Europe. Famous for its stunning architecture dating from Saxon times and including the exceptional Early English West Front, the cathedral has inspired artists and writers down the ages including Lewis Carroll and the poet Wilfred Owen.

Ripon
Ripon Races
Theme: Horse Racing
Directions: On the B6265 Boroughbridge road.
Tel: 01765 602 156
E-mail: info@ripon-races.co.uk
www: ripon-races.co.uk
Children: Welcome.
Disabled: Facilities for disabled visitors.
Dogs: Not allowed.
Facilities: Car parking (FREE), bars, restaurants, shops, playgrounds and family attractions. Also giant screen showing all other races of the day.

Charges:

- Club Enclosure   £15.00
- Tattersalls Enclosure   £10.00
- Course Enclosure   £3.50
- Car (up to 4 adult occupants) Into the Course Enclosure   £10.00
- Accompanied children under 16 FREE
- Senior Citizens Tattersalls £7.00

Description: Yorkshire's Garden Racecourse.

Fixtures 2003

Wednesday, 2nd April	2.10pm-5.30pm
Thursday, 17th April	2.10pm-5.00pm
Saturday, 26th April	2.00pm-5.10pm
Sunday, 18th May	2.10pm-4.40pm
Wednesday, 28th May	6.40pm-9.10pm
Wednesday, 18th June	7.00pm-9.30pm
Thursday, 19th June **Ladies Day**	2.00pm-5.40pm
Monday, 7th July	6.50pm-9.20pm
Saturday, 19th July	2.25pm-5.10pm
Monday, 4th August **Children's Day**	2.15pm-4.45pm
Saturday, 16th August	2.20pm-5.05pm
Monday, 25th August **Bank Holiday**	2.20pm-5.05pm
Tuesday, 26th August **Bank Holiday**	2.15pm-4.45pm
Saturday, 30th August	2.15pm-4.45pm
Saturday, 27th September	2.30pm-5.10pm

Ripon
Ripon Spa Gardens

Theme: Garden or Gardens
Directions: Park Street, Ripon.
Description: Winner of a prestigious Green Flag award in 2001. Offers an 18-hole putting course, flat green bowling, 9-hole crazy golf, 3 tennis courts and restaurant facilities. A great place right in the heart of Ripon to enjoy some family fun, serious sport or just a gentle stroll through the beautiful displays to admire the splendid Victorian bandstand.

Ripon
Workhouse Museum of Poor Law

Theme: Museum
Directions: The Museum is in Allhallowgate.
Tel: 01765 690 799
Description: The former Ripon Union Workhouse, refurbished to portray the treatment of 100 years ago.

Rosedale Abbey
Gillies Jones Glass

Theme: Craft Workshop and Shop
Address: Rosedale Abbey, N. Yorks, YO18 8SA
Tel: 01751 417 550

www: www.gilliesjonesglass.co.uk
Description: Blown glass, pure in form and colour individually sand carved with intricate, complex and precise surface designs inspired by the environment.

Scarborough

Description: Scarborough couldn't be further removed from the timeless peace and tranquillity of the coastal villages. It first became famous in 1626 when a Mrs Tomyzin Farrer discovered the medicinal properties of the town's spring waters. To meet the needs of this influx of visitors, the town provided every fashionable amenity, from nightly dancing and gaming tables to afternoon theatre and horse-racing on the sands, as well as a huge range of accommodation. ● The Victorians brought a touch of elegance and glamour to the seaside town, introducing some of the finest formal gardens in Britain, the magnificent Scarborough Spa and the Esplanade. ● Visitors from all over the country and abroad now flock to Scarborough for a taste of a true British holiday beside the sea. • Climb the steep cobbled streets to the top of the cliff for spectacular views across the bay, or browse around the bustling shopping centre and the old town where trade and tourism keep the atmosphere vibrant throughout the year.

There is a **Tourist Information Centre** at Valley Bridge Road, Tel: 01723 373 333

scarboroughtic@scarborough.gov.uk and
www.yorkshirecoast.co.uk/scarb/

Scarborough (East Ayton)
Betton Animal Farm & Visitor Centre

Theme: Farm, Farm Visitor Centre or Farm Shop
Directions: On A170 3 miles west of Scarborough.
Tel: 01723 863143
Description: Set in a traditional Yorkshire farmstead.

Scarborough
Grainary Hotel & Wildlife Farm

Theme: Farm, Farm Visitor Centre or Farm Shop
Address: Harwood Dale, Scarborough, Y013 0DT
Contact:
Tel: 01723 870026
Description: 200 acre Family Farm, Hotel, Tea rooms, Plant Centre. Animals, Meadows, Trails, Play area etc.

Scarborough
Honey Farm
Theme: Exhibition or Education Centre.
Address: East Ayton, Scarborough, YO13 9HT
Tel: 0800 731 6006 or 01723 863 143
Description: World's best exhibition of the Honey Bee to be remembered by all the family & a chance to select from a wide range of natural bee products.

Scarborough
Langdale Quest
Theme : Sport (Off road driving experience)
Address: Langdale Quest, Bickley Rigg Farm, Bickley, Langdale End, Scarborough, North Yorkshire YO13 0LL
Tel: 01723 882 335
Description: UK.'s largest 4x4 off-road driving site. 1 hour, 2 hour, 3 hour and full day adventures.

Scarborough
Llama Trekking
Theme : Trekking
Address: Wellington Lodge Llama, Staintondale, Scarborough, N. Yorks, YO13 0EL
Tel: 01723 871 234
www: www.llamatreks.co.uk
Description: Wide choice of treks all year round taking in the best scenery and sites of interest.

Scarborough
Peasholme Park
Theme: Park or Garden(s)
Description: Early C20 public park designed in a 'japanese' style. Features include: Pagoda, waterfall and cascade,Willow Pattern bridge, oriental statues and a floating bandstand in the lake.

Scarborough (Ravenscar)
Ravenscar Coastal Centre
Theme: Information Centre
Directions: 10 miles north of Scarborough
Tel: 01723 870 138 or 01723 870 423
Description: A National Trust property. Rock pool aquarium and shop. Near to the Peak Alum Works.

Scarborough
Rotunda Museum
Theme : Museum
Address: Vernon Road, Scarborough, YO11 2NN

Tel: 01723 374 839
Description: A new exhibition exploring Scarborough's seaside heritage.

Scarborough
Scarborough Art Gallery
Theme: Arts Gallery or Centre
Address: The Crescent, Scarborough, YO11 2PW
Tel: 01723 374 753
Description: Hands on display telling the story of Scarborough from fishing village to fashionable resort.

Scarborough
Scarborough Castle
Theme : Castle or Castle Ruins
Directions: East of the town centre on Castle Road
Tel: 01723 372 451
Description: 12th century fortress with a huge keep, over three storeys high with breathtaking views.

Scarborough
Scarborough Millennium
Theme: Local History
Address: Harbourside, Scarborough, YO11 1PG
Tel: 01723 501000
Description: Local history brought alive in a refreshing new way that both children and adults can enjoy.

Scarborough
Scarborough Sea Life & Marine Sanctuary
Theme: Marine Attraction (Conservation & Rescue)
Address: Scalby Mills, Scarborough, YO12 6RP
Tel: 01723 376 125
Description: World of the Octopus, Seal Pool, Turtles, Otters, Kingdom of the Seahorse and Seal Hospital.

Scarborough
Stained Glass Centre
Theme: Craft Workshop or Shop
Directions: Just off the B1261 between the villages of Cayton and Lebberston.
Tel: 01723 581 236 or 01723 585 465
www: www.stainedglass-centre.co.uk
Description: Learn about the history of stained glass and browse in the showrooms.

Scarborough
Staintondale Shire Horse Farm
Theme: Farm, Farm Visitor Centre or Farm Shop
Address: Staintondale, Scarborough, Y013 OEY
Tel: 01723 870458
Description: Paradise for horse and pony lovers. Live shows take place on days each week the farm is open.

Scarborough
Stephen Joseph Theatre
Theme: Theatre or Playhouse
Address: Westborough, Scarborough, YO11 1JW
Tel: 01723 370 541
Description: Founded in Scarborough by theatrical pioneer Stephen Joseph.

Scarborough
Wood End Museum
Theme : Museum
Address: The Crescent, Scarborough, YO11 2PW
Tel: 01723 367 326
Description: Large-scale artworks to stimulate the senses, exploring the natural world.

Sedbergh
Facilities: Parking and Toilets at the National Park Centre car park.
Description: Just 5 miles East of the M6 Motorway, Junction 37 and midway between Hawes and Kendal. • The attractive old market town of Sedbergh, with its cobbled yards and unique atmosphere, is not only set in the magnificent western dales of North Yorkshire but also close to the rugged eastern fells of the Lake District. • Developed at a confluence of four valleys and four rivers where ancient trade routes merged, the town is dwarfed by some of Alfred Wainwright's favourite fells, the mighty Howgills. The views from all around the area are stunning. • For those who like to explore there are many narrow lanes and small clusters of old dwellings worthy of close inspection: there is a fine Norman Church; while overlooking the town, high above Settlebeck to the east of the town, is the site of **Castlehaw**, an ancient motte and bailey castle built to repel the rebellious Scottish hordes. • For the serious walker there are the magnificent Howgill Fells and the Dales Way walk. • Approximately 5 miles east of Sedbergh is Cautley Spout, a plunging cascade which falls some 200m down Cautley Crag to. • Guided walks of the town and Sedbergh School are available during the summer whilst cyclists have the Cumbrian

Cycleway, a 250 mile circular route which passes through and can be joined at Sedbergh. ● George Fox, founder of the Quakers, preached in both St. Andrews churchyard and the nearby **Briggflatts Quaker Meeting House**, which dates from 1675 and is the oldest meeting house in the North of England. ● Attractions include **Farfield Clothing**, **Dent Crafts Centre** and Gallery and **Farfield Mill** Arts and Heritage Centre.

There is a Tourist Information Centre at 72, Main Street. Try

sedbergh@yorkshiredales.org.uk

Sedbergh (Dent)
Dent Crafts Centre
Theme: Craft Centre & Gallery

Directions: On the main road between Sedbergh and Dent. 8 miles from the M6 exit 37.
Address: Helmside, Dent, Cumbria, LAIO 5SY
Contact: Carrol & Joe Stephenson
Tel: 015396 25400
Fax: 015396 25400
E-mail: carrol@dentcraftcentre.fsnet.co.uk
www:
www.whitehousedentdale.btinternet.co.uk/CraftCentre/
Disabled: Help available for wheel-chair users.
Dogs: Welcome.
Parking: There is ample parking for visitors.
Toilets: Available on site
Refreshments: The tearoom displays a captivating collection of tools of yesteryear. Enjoy morning coffee, light lunch or afternoon tea, outside in the garden, or inside by the fire. Home-baked cakes and cookies, teas and fresh ground coffee are a popular treat. Freshly filled baps, homemade wholesome soups and delicious ice cream, made in the Dales.
Shop: Enticing collection including puzzle boxes, bird sculptures, walking sticks and wooden bowls. ● Handmade cards, silk flowers, wool tops, waistcoats and travel rugs in Yorkshire wool. ● Pottery and ceramics from local studios, original water- colours, prints, silver jewellery, creative metalwork, country antique corner and much more.

Open: Six days a week Easter to November • 10-30am
- 5.00pm • Closed Tuesdays.
Winter Hours • weekends, Christmas and New Year
Holidays (except Christmas Day) • Closed early
January to mid February • Otherwise phone for times.
Description: The Gallery, converted from an eighteenth
century hay barn is a perfect setting for the display of
watercolours, crafts and prints many by artists and
crafts people of the Dales.

Sedbergh
Farfield Clothing
Theme: Shopping (Outdoor clothing)
Address: The Old School, Joss Lane, LA10 5AS
Tel: 01539 620 629
Description: International reputation for producing
quality outdoor clothing. Designed for the whole family.

Sedbergh
Farfield Mill
Theme: Arts & Heritage Centre
Directions: On the A684 Garsdale – Hawes Road just
one mile east of Sedbergh. Look for the *AA* signs.
Only 30mins from Hawes, Kirkby Stephen, Kendal,
Penrith & Kirkby Lonsdale.
Address: Garsdale Road, Sedbergh, LA10 5LW
Tel: 015396 21958
E-mail: themanager@farfieldmill.org
www: www.farfieldmill.org
Children: Welcome when accompanied by an adult.
Disabled: Facilities available throughout.
Dogs: If well behaved and by permission of Centre
Manager on the day.
Parking: Ample car parking is available – Coaches
welcome, by appointment only.
Refreshments: A quality café – coffee and much more
available.
Facilities: The mill is situated beside the beautiful River
Clough where advantage can be taken of many
delightful walks.
Open: 7th April 2003 – 11th Jan 2004 - Seven Days per
Week 10.30 am – 5.00 pm. - Closed Christmas Day &
Boxing Day – Open New Years Day. • 12th Jan 2004 –
4th April 2004 - Saturdays & Sundays only.
• Last admission 4.30 pm.
Charges: Adults £2, Senior Citizens & Students £1.50,
Children FREE. Group rates on application.
Description: A restored building via the efforts of local
volunteer enthusiasts. • Originally a Woollen Mill dating
back to about 1835. • Experience local people creating
stunning and unique pieces of work in their own studios
including Artist / Painter, Photographer, Potter, Weaver,

Felt maker, Woodwork, Knitwear, Ceramics, Glass, Silk / Velvet, Pewter. • See a changing programme throughout the year of fine quality exhibitions. • Also view displays that explain the history of the Mill and some of its workers and local inhabitants. • See the two renovated Victorian Dobcross Looms, which can often be observed working. Additionally you can purchase products made on them from the Mill Shop amongst many other items produced in the Centre.

Selby
Selby Abbey

Theme: Abbey or Abbey Ruins
Description: Benedict of Auxerre, France founded the abbey after he was directed in a vision to a place called Selebaie - the Sallow village. With the permission of William the Conqueror he chose this place as the site for his abbey. • The Benedictine abbey was built in typical Norman style. Its internal architecture is similar to Durham Cathedral. In the Dissolution of the monasteries Selby was lucky enough to escape and although part was pulled down the central nave survived. In 1618 it became the parish church of Selby.

Selby
Yorkshire Garden World

Theme: Garden or Gardens
Directions: Easily accessible from the M62 and the A1.
Tel: 01757 228279
www: www.yorkshiregardenw.f9.co.uk
Description: 14 beautiful display and nursery gardens set in 6 acres of rural North Yorkshire. Large tearoom.

Settle (Rathmell)
Northern Equine Therapy Centre

Theme: Farm, Farm Visitor Centre or Farm Shop
Address: Rathmell, Settle, North Yorkshire, BD24 OLA
Tel: 01729 840 284
Description: Unique opportunity to see how therapy is given to horses: including the equine swimming pool.

Settle
Pen-y-ghent

Theme: Land or Seascape
Description: The lowest of the Three Peaks (see also Ingleborough (p35) and Whernside (p61)) at 2,277 feet (694m). The most frequented route is 3 miles (4.8km) each way from Horton village. Once up there, walkers can revel in the views. Looking north, trains can be seen moving northwards from Horton towards Whernside. It is built up of a millstone grit cap resting on limestone.

Settle
Settle to Carlisle Railway

Theme: Scenic Railway
Tel: 01729 825 037 or 08457 48 49 50
www: www.settle-carlisle.co.uk
Open: Daily services and occasional specials.
Description: Completed for passenger travel in 1876. One of the feats of Victorian engineering it required 72 miles of track, 20 major viaducts and 14 tunnels. From Leeds to Skipton and Settle then on through the heart of the "Three Peaks" country, over the soaring Ribble viaduct and on to the Eden Valley to finish at Carlisle.

Settle
Watershed Mill Visitor Centre

Theme: Visitor Centre
Directions: Off the A65, large car park. 5 minutes walk from Settle.
Tel: 01729 825 539
www: www.watershedmill.co.uk
Disabled: Disabled access and facilities.
Dogs: Allowed but Guide dogs only in Coffee Shop.
Parking: Free parking on site
Toilets: Toilets on site
Refreshments: 82 seat Licensed coffee shop.
Open: • Mon - Sat 10:00am to 5:30pm • Sun 11:00am - 5:00pm • Open all year except Christmas day & Easter Sunday •
Description: Whether visiting the Yorkshire Dales for the day or Watershed Mill is the place for enjoyment for all ages in all weathers. • Nestling beneath the largest outcrop of limestone in Britain on the banks of the River Ribble, Watershed Mill, once an 1820's cotton mill has been converted into a Visitor Centre in the market town of Settle. • The famous Settle-Carlisle Railway passes only a few hundred yards from the door and Settle is the perfect base to explore the line. • The Edinburgh Woollen Mill • The Dalesmade Centre • The Rock & Fossil Shop • The Golf Shop • Country Kitchen Coffee

Shop ● Yorkshire Real Ale and Whisky Shop (free tastings) ● Food and Gift Emporium.

Settle
Yorkshire Dales Falconry & Conservation Centre

Theme: Conservation
Directions: Signposted off the A65 bypass from Settle to Kendal. The Centre is situated beside the bypass.
Tel: 01729 822 832 or 01729 825 164
Description: Many of the world's Birds of Prey are under threat of extinction. Successful captive breeding and educational programmes will safeguard them for future generations.

Sheffield

Description: Sheffield has all that you would expect and more from England's fourth largest city. ● It is the country's greenest city. The beautiful Peak National Park, ideal for walking and climbing, is right on the doorstep. ● Top names in rock and pop perform at Don Valley Stadium and Sheffield Arena. Sheffield has an outstanding calendar of festivals and entertainment. The Crucible, Lyceum and Studio form the largest theatrical complex outside London. ● Sheffield was Britain's first National City of Sport and boasts some of the best international sports venues in the country. Visitor attractions include the **Bishops' House** and the **Millennium Galleries**. There is a Tourist Information Centre at Tudor Square. Tel 0114 221 1900. Try **visitor@sheffield.gov.uk**

Sheffield
Abbeydale Industrial Hamlet

Theme: Museum
Directions: About 4 miles from city centre on the A621.
Tel: 0114 272 2106
E-mail: feedback@simt.co.uk
www: www.simt.co.uk
Description: A steel working site with a long history. Find out about the people who lived and worked here.

Sheffield
Bishops' House

Theme: Museum
Directions: From the city centre take the A61 to Chesterfield. Turn left up Derbyshire Lane and left onto Norton Lees Lane.
Bus No. 13 and 39 from the city centre.

Address: Bishops' House, Meersbrook Park, Norton Lees Lane, Sheffield, S8 9BE
Tel: 0114 278 2600
www: sheffieldgalleries.org.uk
Disabled: Upper floor not accessible to wheelchair users.
Parking: On street.
Refreshments: No.
Open:
- Sat   10am - 4.30pm
- Sun   11am - 4.30pm.

Charges: Admission: FREE
Description: Bishops' House dates from around 1500 and is the best preserved timber-framed house in Sheffield. Many original features survive, and the Bedchamber and Great Parlour are furnished in the style of the home of a prosperous 17th century yeoman.

Sheffield
Cathedral Church of St Peter and St Paul

Theme: Cathedral or Cathedral Ruins
Address: Church Street, Sheffield, S1 1HA
Tel: 0114 275 3434
Description: Originally built in about 1430 in the perpendicular gothic style.

Sheffield
Kelham Island Museum

Theme: Museum
Tel: 0114 272 2106 **Fax:** 0114 275 7847
E-mail: feedback@simt.co.uk
www: www.simt.co.uk
Description: Tells the story of Sheffield and its people in the cutlery, toolmaking and silverware trades.

Sheffield
Millennium Galleries

Theme: Art Gallery
Directions: Situated in the centre of Sheffield on Arundel Gate, opposite Sheffield Hallam University and next to the Novotel. ● From the M1 leave at junction 33 and take the A57 to Sheffield. Follow signs for the city centre and the theatres. ● 5-10 minutes walk from the railway station. Leave the station, cross the road and walk straight up Howard Street, by Sheffield Hallam University. You will be able to see the Millennium Galleries at the top of the hill. ● There is a coach drop off point close to the entrance on Arundel Gate at the rear of the Central Library and Graves Art Gallery. ●

The Millennium Galleries is easily reached from any city centre bus and tram stop.

Address: Millennium Galleries, Arundel Gate, Sheffield, S1 2PP

Tel: 0114 278 2600

Fax: 0114 278 2604

www: www.sheffieldgalleries.org.uk

Disabled: Fully accessible.

Dogs: Guide dogs allowed.

Parking: There is plenty of car parking across the city. The closest is the NCP car park at the Crucible Theatre. Visitors to the Millennium Galleries are able to park here at a reduced rate of £3 for 3 hours. A voucher will be issued upon request and on production of a valid car park ticket at the Millennium Galleries reception.

Refreshments: Café Azure is open during gallery opening hours and serves an excellent selection of high quality meals and light refreshments.

Shop: The gallery shop sells a wide range of cards, posters, pictures, magazines, gifts and other items related to the exhibitions.

Open:

- Monday – Saturday   10am - 5pm
- Sunday   11am - 5pm

Charges:

- Admission to the Millennium Galleries is FREE.
- There is an admission charge to special exhibitions.
- Pre-booked groups of 10 or more can get a 10% discount on entry to the Special Exhibition Gallery. For more information please call 0114 278 2655.

Description: The Millennium Galleries is home to the Ruskin Gallery and Sheffield's internationally important metalwork collection. Blockbuster exhibitions for 2003 include Constable, Flower Power and Pleasure Land. The Craft and Design Gallery shows a range of contemporary and historical exhibitions.

Sheffield
Shepherd Wheel

Theme: Museum

Tel: 0114 272 2106   **Fax:** 0114 275 7847

E-mail: feedback@simt.co.uk

www: www.simt.co.uk

Description: A good example of Sheffield's industrial past, which was dependent on the skills of its cutlers.

Skipton

www: www.skiptononline.co.uk

Description: Settled by sheep farmers as long ago as the 7th century it is today known as the "Gateway to the Dales". Guarded today by its magnificent **Skipton**

Castle it is a major commercial and shopping centre with a colourful market 4 days a week (Monday, Wednesday, Friday and Saturday) and a variety of interesting pubs and eating places. Other nearby visitor attractions include the **Embsay and Bolton Abbey Steam Railway**. There is a Tourist Information Centre at Coach Street, Tel. 01756 792 809. Try **skipton@ytbtic.co.uk**.

Skipton
Balloon Flights over the Yorkshire Dales
Theme: Balloon Flights
Tel: 01756 730 166
Description: Flights daily from Settle or Skipton.

Skipton
Craven Museum
Theme: Museum
Address: Town Hall, High Street, Skipton, BD23 1AH
Tel: 01756 796 407
Description: History of the Southern Dales.

Skipton
Embsay and Bolton Abbey Steam Railway
Theme: Scenic Railway
Directions: Embsay is 2 miles from Skipton, signposted from the A59. Bolton Abbey Station, on the A59, is 7 miles from Ilkley.

Tel: 01756 710614. **Talking Timetable:** 01756 795189
E-mail: embsay.steam@btinternet.com
www: www.embsayboltonabbeyrailway.org.uk
Children: Welcome. Baby changing facilities at both stations.

Disabled: Welcome. Ramp access is available to all normal trains. Disabled toilet facilities at Bolton Abbey Station only at present.

Dogs: Welcome.
Parking: Parking on site.

Toilets: Toilets at both stations but disabled facilities at Bolton Abbey Station only at present.

Refreshments: Refreshments available at both stations.

Shop: At both stations.

Open: Sundays and up to 7 days a week in Summer; all year 10:00am to 5:00 pm (4:00pm in winter).

Charges: 2003 - return fares

Adults: £6; Children: £3.00; Concessions: £5; Family Ticket: £16 (2 Adults & 2 Children).

Description: Scenic steam railway along 5 miles of track through picturesque Yorkshire Dales scenery.

- Trains run between the new award winning Bolton Abbey Station and Embsay Station, bult in 1888. Visits from Thomas the Tank Engine at Easter, Spring and August Bank Hoilidays. Yorkshire's friendly line.
- Bolton Abbey Station is an ideal dropping off point for a pleasant 1.5 mile walk to the ruins of the historic 12th century Priory or to the river walks alongside the Wharfe.

Skipton
Gardenmakers

Theme: Garden Design and Plant Centre

Directions: South of Wigglesworth on the Bolton by Bowland road. Follow Wigglesworth or brown "Flower" signs from A65 near Settle or "Gardenmakers" signs from A59 at Sawley

Tel: 01729 840 848

www: gardenmakers.co.uk

Refreshments: The Grubbery offers tasty meals, teas etc with fresh home baked bread, scones and hand made cakes.

Shop: The Outlook offers a range of gifts from the unusual to the very practical. In **The Summerhouse** you will find a useful array of gardening essentials.

Open: 9.00am – 5.30pm every day.

Description: A unique gardener's paradise situated in glorious countryside. Designed to provide inspiration and good practical advice, it also has one of the finest collections of plants in the North with over 2,000 varieties of hardy plants, trees, shrubs etc, including many unusual ones.

Skipton
Skipton Castle

Theme: Castle
Directions: At the upper end of the High Street
Tel: 01756 792 442
E-mail: info@skiptoncastle.co.uk
www: www.skiptoncastle.co.uk
Children: Welcome including school parties
Disabled: No access to medieval castle
Dogs: On a lead please
Parking: Parking in town car park 5 minutes walk from the Castle
Toilets: Toilets on site
Refreshments: Tearoom serves cream teas and light meals
Open: Every day – except 25th December.

- Open 10:00am (Sundays 12:00 noon).
- Last admissions 6:00pm (Oct - Feb 4:00pm).

Charges:

- Adults: £4.80 with illustrated tour sheet
- Under 18s: £2.40 with illustrated tour sheet
- Under 5s: FREE
- Over 60s and students: £4.20 with illustrated tour sheet
- Family Ticket for two adults and up to 3 children under 18: £13.50
- Illustrated tour sheets in choice of 8 languages.
- Guides are available for pre-booked parties at no extra cost. Adult parties of 15 or more: £3.90 per head
- School parties (all ages): £2.40 per head (supervising teachers free)

Events: 2003:
24th – 26th May The Red Wyvern Society will re-enact life during the Wars of the Roses.
26th – 27th July Life & Times will re-enact scenes from The English Civil War.
16th - 17th August The Feudal Archers - a 12th century medieval display and encampment.
Description: One of the most complete and well preserved medieval castles in England, over 900 years old.
Ten turbulent centuries of English history with the Clifford Lords fighting at Bannockburn, Agincourt and in

the Wars of the Roses, has seen Skipton Castle standing as guardian of the gateway to the Yorkshire Dales. Founded around 1090 by Robert de Romille, one of William the Conqueror's Barons, it became the stronghold of the Clifford Lords in 1310. During the Civil War it was the last Royalist bastion in the North, yielding only after a three-year siege in 1645. On the orders of Cromwell, it was 'slighted' but later skilfully restored by the redoubtable Lady Anne Clifford who planted the yew tree in the beautiful Tudor courtyard in 1659.

A unique fortress, standing today complete and well-preserved on a 40-metre high crag above this bustling market town. Every period has left its mark, with its Norman entrance, Medieval towers, dungeon, the ancient Chapel of St John the Evangelist and the Shell Room decorated in the 1620s with shells and Jamaican coral.

Thirsk
Beaver Furniture
Theme: Craft Workshop or Shop
Address: Colin Almack, Beaver Lodge, Sutton-under-Whitestone Cliff, Thirsk, North Yorkshire, Y07 2PR
Tel: 01845 597 420
Description: Established in 1960 this family-run business embodies the very best in craftsman-made furniture, symbolised by the unique beaver trademark.

Thirsk (Byland)
Byland Abbey
Theme: Abbey or Abbey Ruins
Directions: 11 miles from Thirsk, 2 from Coxwold.
Tel: 01347 868 614
Description: An English Heritage property. Haunting ruin of large and prosperous Cistercian abbey.

Thirsk
Design in Wood
Theme: Craft Workshop or Shop
Directions: The Old Coach House, Chapel Street
Tel: 01845 525010 **Fax:** 01845 523092
www: www.designinwood.co.uk
Description: Imaginatively designed high quality freestanding and fitted furniture.

Thirsk
English Hardwood Furniture
Theme: Craft Workshop or Shop
Address: The Mill Yard, Catton Lane, Topcliffe, Thirsk.
Tel: 01845 578 172
Description: Workshop on the banks of the River Swale combining traditional and innovative designs.

Thirsk
Fox Furniture
Theme: Craft Workshop or Shop
Directions: Carlton Husthwaite, 6 miles South of Thirsk
Tel: 01845 501359
Description: Traditional handmade furniture from English oak and other hardwoods

Thirsk
Monk Park Farm Visitor Centre
Theme: Farm, Farm Visitor Centre or Farm Shop
Directions: $\frac{1}{2}$ mile off A-170 East of Thirsk.
Tel: 01845 597 730 or 01845 597 412
www: www.monkpark.co.uk
Description: Wide range of animals with indoor and outdoor feeding areas ● Tearoom & Toilets ●

Thirsk (Kilburn)
Mouseman of Kilburn
Theme: Craft Workshop or Shop
Directions: From Thirsk take A170 road, turn right after two miles, follow signs to Kilburn. Turn right at the T-junction. Showroom on the left, 50 yards from junction.
Tel: 01347 869 100 **Fax:** 01347 869 103
E-mail: info@robertthompsons.co.uk
www: www.robertthompsons.co.uk
Description: Domestic and ecclesiastical furniture bearing world famous mouse trademark.

Thirsk
Old Mill Furniture
Theme: Craft Workshop or Shop
Directions: At Balk, 4 miles East of Thirsk off the A170.
Tel: 01845 597 227
Description: Domestic furniture in solid oak, walnut, maple, mahogany, cherry, elm, chestnut and ash in traditional, timeless and modem styles.

Thirsk
Ritz Cinema

Theme: Cinema or Cinema Complex
Address: 16, Westgate, Thirsk, N. Yorks, YO7 1QS
Tel: 01845 524 751
www: www.ritzcinema.co.uk
Description: Traditional local cinema showing up to date releases. Run by volunteers for the benefit of the local community and visitors alike.

Thirsk (Kirby Wiske)
Sion Hill Hall

Theme: House or House & Garden
Address: Kirby Wiske, Thirsk, N. Yorks, YO7 4EU
Tel: 01845 587 206
Description: One of the best country houses to be constructed during the Edwardian era.

Thirsk
Thirsk Races

Theme: Horse Racing
Directions: Situated just west of Thirsk Town centre on the A61 to Ripon (Station Road). Thirsk Station is only half a mile from the racecourse entrances.

Address: Thirsk Racecourse Ltd., Station Road, Thirsk, North Yorkshire, YO7 1QL
Tel: 01845 522 276 **Fax:** 01845 525 353
E-mail: info@thirskraces.fsnet.co.uk
www: www.thirskracecourse.net
Disabled: All facilities are suitable for the disabled.
Dogs: No! Guide dogs for the blind only please.
Parking: Ample FREE car and coach parking.
Toilets: On site including facilities for the disabled.
Refreshments: Wide choice of facilities.
Shop: On site
Facilities: Private viewing boxes available.
Open: Please ring for meeting dates. April to September.
Charges:
● **Club**: £15 ● **Tattersalls**: £10; (OAP) £5 ● **Family Ring**: £3; (OAP) £1.50; Cars into Family Ring (including up to four adults) £10; Holders of disabled badge: £5.
● **Concessions for pre-booked parties**
● **Club**: 20+: £14 ● **Tattersalls**: 20+: £9 ● **Family Ring**: 20+: £2.50. ● **Tattersalls**: 100+: £8.50 ● **Family Ring**: 100+: £2. **Plus** one FREE badge for every 20 Tattersalls or Family Ring tickets purchased.

- **Annual membership**: *Single*: £120; *Joint*: £200; *Junior* (aged 17-21): £40.
- Accompanied children under 16 years of age are admitted **FREE** of charge.
- Dress Code for Club Enclosure - collared shirt and tie.

Description: The Hambleton area of North Yorkshire, set between the North Yorkshire Moors and the Dales, is steeped in equine history, with racing taking place back in 1740. There has been racing on the present site since 1855.

Thirsk
Treske

Theme: Craft Workshop or Shop (Solid wood furniture)
Directions: On the A61, close to the railway station.
Tel: 01845 522770
www: www.treske.co.uk
Description: Solid Ash, beech, cherry, elm, maple, oak, sycamore and yew are durable, look lovely and have beautiful natural colours.

Thirsk (Kilburn)
White Horse of Kilburn

Theme: Scenic View, Walk or Ride
Directions: Follow the signs from the A170 road.
Description: Huge, turf cut figure on the hillside near the village. Can be seen from 40 miles away. Cut in 1857 it is 228ft high and 312ft long.

Thirsk
World of James Herriot

Theme: Museum
Directions: In the centre of Thirsk at 23, Kirkgate.
www: www.worldofjamesherriot.org
Description: The veterinary surgery and house made famous by the author James Herriot. Social and veterinary history, nostalgia, science, education, humour and fun.

Wakefield
National Coal Mining Museum for England

Theme: Museum
Address: Caphouse Colliery, New Road, Overton.
Tel: 01924 848 806
Description: The underground tour goes 140 metres underground and traces mining conditions through time.

Wakefield
Nostell Priory
Theme: House & Garden
Directions: On the A638, 5 miles SE of Wakefield.
Tel: 01924 863 892
Description: A National Trust property. One of Yorkshire's finest jewels. An 18th century architectural masterpiece. Houses one of England's finest collections of Chippendale furniture. Delightful lakeside walks.

Wakefield
Sandal Castle
Theme: Castle or Castle Ruins
Description: In a commanding position overlooking the River Calder. Best known for the Battle of Wakefield fought nearby in 1460 during the Wars of the Roses. Richard, Duke of York was killed. During the Civil War Sandal Castle was besieged twice by Parliamentary forces. Afterwards, it was stripped of its defences. Remains of the 13th century stone castle and the fine motte and bailey can be seen on site.

Wetherby
Description: Charming historic town on the banks of the River Wharfe. Originally a staging post midway between London and Edinburgh. Now a busy market town, still retaining its Thursday Market, granted by Royal Charter in 1240. There are many specialist shops in the town, including high class gifts, glass, pottery, furniture, art galleries, book shop, sewing, tapestry and needlework centre, delicatessens, a saddlery, quality shoe stores and jewellers.
There ia a Tourist Information Centre at the Council Offices, 24 Westgate, Tel. 0113 247 7251 or visit **www.leeds.gov.uk**.

Wetherby
Bramham Park
Theme: Garden(s)
Address: Bramham Park, Wetherby.
Tel: 01937 846 000
Description: Early 18th Century French style formal gardens, almost unique in England.

Whitby
Captain Cook Memorial Museum
Theme: Museum (Maritime History and Historic Building)
Directions: Town Centre, near swing bridge.

Address: Grape Lane, Whitby, N. Yorks, YO22 4BA
Tel and Fax: 01947 601 900
www: www.cookmuseumwhitby.co.uk
Open: • **March:** Weekends 11:00am to 3:00pm
• **April to End of October:** DAILY 09:45am to 5:00pm
Description: Harbourside house (17th c) to which
James Cook came as apprentice • Attic where he
lodged • Rich collections: paintings, drawings and
original artefacts from the Voyages, letters in Cook's
hand and other original manuscripts, period rooms,
ships plans and models • Recently extended.

Whitby
Frank Meadow Sutcliffe Gallery
Theme: Arts Gallery or Centre
Description: Photographs recall the Victorian era.
Portraits of bearded lifeboatmen and waif-like fishergirls
contrast with idyllic harvest scenes and a study of
Whitby Abbey shrouded in mist.

Whitby (Robin Hood's Bay)
Old Coastguard Station
Theme: Exhibition or Education Centre.
Directions: Next to the slipway overlooking the bay.
Tel: 01947 885 900
Description: National Trust property. Restored to its
19th Century appearance as a coastal lookout station.

Whitby
Whitby Abbey
Theme: Abbey or Abbey Ruins
Directions: On the clifftop east of the town centre.
Tel: 01947 603 568
Open: All year.
Description: The Benedictine church built in the 13th
and 14th centuries dominates the headland and stands
on the site of the monastery founded in 657, home of
St. Hilda and Caedmon, the first English hymn writer.

Withernsea
Withernsea Lighthouse
Theme: Lighthouse
Address: Hull Road, Withernsea, E. Yorks HU19 2DY
Tel: 01964 614834
Refreshments: Café provides a welcome cup of tea
and light refreshments.
Shop: Souvenirs are on sale.
Description: Towers 127 feet above the town. The
Base features many exhibits including a local history
section. Views from the lamproom are breathtaking.

York

Description: Reputedly one of the most intriguing cities in England. The superbly preserved walled city has witnessed more than 2,000 years of vibrant history. ● Attractions include the largest Gothic cathedral in northern Europe, the magnificent **York Minster,** the **National Railway Museum**, the **Castle Museum** with its perfectly recreated Victorian and Edwardian streets, the terrifying **York Dungeon**, the new £5 million **Jorvik**, which 'flies' you through time and **Castle Howard**, one of Britain's finest stately homes. ● For a Guided Tour you may choose from the **Ghost Trail of York** (p126), the **Haunted Walk of York** (p127), **Yorkwalk** (p140), a visit to **York Brewery** (p134) or enjoy the City sights aboard a guided river trip with **YorkBoat** (p139) or atop an open **York City Sightseeing** (p135) bus. ● The history of two of Yorkshire's famous regiments is to be found at the **Regimental Museum** (p130) and if walking the City Walls you must visit the **Micklegate Bar Museum** (p129) or the **Richard III Museum** (p131). ● Neither the **Friargate Theatre** (p126) or the **York Shakespeare Project** (p139) should be missed, **Stillingfleet Lodge Garden and Nursery** (p133) is packed with plants and foliage and **York Model Railway** (p138) is for adults and children alike. **Barley Hall** (p123) is a medieval town house right in the centre of the city and the **Yorvik Brass Rubbing Centre** (p141) is only 5 minutes from the centre. On the outskirts of the city there are the **York Maize Maze** (p137) with over 5 miles of pathways to get lost in and the North's Premier indoor Karting venue at **F1 Racing - Premier Karting** (p125). ● For those who love to shop, York offers a first-class opportunity to browse in traditional gift shops, independent boutiques and investigate curios and antiques. **Mulberry Hall** (p129) is one of the world's leading china, porcelain, crystal, enamels, silver and cookware specialists.

There is a Tourist Information Centre at the De Grey Rooms, Exhibition Square and at York Railway Station Tel: 01904-621756 or visit **www.visityork.org**

York
Battle of Marston Moor
Theme: Battle. Site of
Directions: Between Long Marston and Tockwith.
Description: July 2nd, 1644. Turning point in the Civil War with a victory for the Parliamentary forces. Field marked by obelisk and information board.

York
Bettys Café Tea Rooms
Theme: Refreshments
Address: Bettys, 6-8 St. Helens Square and Little Bettys, 46 Stonegate, York.
Tel: Bettys 01904 659142 and Little Bettys 622865
www: www.bettysandtaylors.co.uk
Description: A visit to one of Bettys Cafè Tea Rooms is a must. An oasis of elegance and calm. Famous for its tea and cakes you can also try a selection of Yorkshire and Swiss dishes. Everything they serve is made by hand.

York
Bar Convent Museum
Theme: Museum/Gallery
Address: 17 Blossom Street, York
Tel: 01904 643238
Description: Outlines the early history of Christianity in the North of England

York
Barley Hall
Theme: Historic Building
Directions: Barley Hall is located on Coffee Yard, which runs between Grape Lane and Stonegate
Address: Barley Hall, 2 Coffee Yard, York, YO1 8AR
Contact: Gill Page
Tel: 01904 610275
Fax: 01904 653848
E-mail: barley.hall@btclick.com
www: www.barleyhall.org.uk
Disabled: Access is limited to the ground floor. FREE admission for wheelchair users.
Shop: Selling quality replicas of medieval crafts.
Facilities: Splendid audio tour available, featuring Judi Dench and Robert Hardy. Costumed tours available for pre-booked groups. Barley Hall is a splendid venue for small dinners, receptions, banquets or a wedding, lying as it does in the centre of historic York.

The Great Hall

Open: March to October: 10am to 4pm, Tuesday to Sunday. **November to February**: 12 noon to 4pm Tuesday to Sunday.

Charges:
- Adult: £3.50
- Child: £2.50 Accompanied under 10s FREE
- Family: £10.00
- Concession: £2.50
- Senior Citizen: £2.50

Description: Barley Hall is a unique survival in York, a city of wonderful buildings. It is a medieval building in the centre of the city, forgotten until a few years ago, concealed as it was under a jumble of run down derelict offices and workshops.

Excavation in the 1980s revealed that under this jumble was a surviving example of a medieval town house, originally the town house of the Priors of Nostell but later to be the town house of its best known inhabitant, Alderman William Snawsell, goldsmith and Mayor of York. It has been restored to how it looked at the time of Alderman Snawsell, towards the end of the fifteenth century, and it is now possible to tour the hall and see how people lived then.

York (Beningbrough)
Beningbrough Hall & Gardens

Theme: House & Garden
Directions: 8 miles NW of York off the A19.
Tel: 01094 470 666
Description: A National Trust Property. Fine, red-brick, Georgian house, built in 1716. Contains one of the most impressive baroque interiors in England.

York (Castle Howard)
Castle Howard

Theme: House or House & Garden
Directions: Signposted from the B1257 & the A64
Tel: 01653 648 444
www: www.castlehoward.co.uk
Description: One of Britain's finest stately homes. Built in 1699 it is still the private home of the Howard family. Inside there are collections of art treasures, antique sculpture and porcelain whilst outside there are gardens, lakes, fountains and temples to admire.

York
Castle Museum

Theme: Museum
Directions: close to Clifford's Tower.
Tel: 08457 660 280 01904 653 611

Description: A unique combination of everyday life and extraordinary objects. Famous for some of the finest collections in the country: the military collection, the social history collection and the costume collection.

York
Clifford's Tower
Theme: Castle or Castle Ruins
Directions: Opposite the Castle Museum
Tel: 01904 646 940
Description: An English Heritage property. The original wooden tower was one of two Norman castles built to help William the Conqueror subdue the North.

York (Stockton-on-the-Forest)
Craven Collection of Classic Motorcycles
Theme: Museum (Motoring Memorabilia)
Address: Brockfield Villa, Stockton-on-the-Forest, York, YO32 9UE
Tel: 01904 488 461 or 01904 400 493
Description: Private collection of over 200 vintage and post-war motorcycles and motoring memorabilia.

York
F1 Racing – Premier Karting
Theme: Recreation (Karting)
Directions: Located on York's only leisure park at Monks Cross.
Address: F1 Racing, Monks Cross, York, YO32 9JS
Tel: 01904 673555
Fax: 01904 626285
E-mail: f1.racing@btopenworld.com
www: www.karting.uk.com
Children: Minimum age 10 yrs - Minimum height 1.4m.
Parking: Secure parking with CCTV.
Refreshments: Fully licensed bar.
Open:
- Monday to Friday: 11am - 7pm
- Saturday and Sunday: 10am - 7pm
- Open outside these hours for pre-booked groups.

Description: The North's Premier indoor Karting venue - Ideal for corporate & group events.

York
Fairfax House
Theme : Museum
Address: Fairfax House, Castlegate, York, YO1 9RN
Tel: 01904 655 543 **Fax:** 01904 652 262

www: www.fairfaxhouse.co.uk
Description: One of the finest 18th c townhouses and home of the famous Noel Terry collection of furniture.

York (Brandsby)
Farming Flashback
Theme: Museum (Farming bygones)
Directions: Thorpe Hall Farm, between Yearsley & Ampleforth, 18 miles N of York on the B1363
Tel: 01439 788 793
Description: Over 100 years of farming history collected & displayed by the Redhead family.

York
Friargate Theatre
Theme: Theatre or Playhouse
Address: Lower Friargate, off Clifford Street, York, YO1 9SL
Contact: Jonathan Brown, General Manager.
Tel: Visitors Booking Line 0845 961 3000 (all calls charged at local rates)
Fax: 01904 651532
E-mail: info@rltc.org
www: www.ridinglights.org
Refreshments: Licensed bar.
Charges: Admission charges vary.
Awards: York Tourism Bureau "Best Entertainment" 2002
Description: Vibrant studio theatre, owned and managed by Riding Lights Theatre Company, hosting touring productions by Riding Lights and a variety of events by visiting performing arts groups. Programme details from the box office.

York
Ghost Hunt of York
Theme: Ghosts and Ghouls
Tel: 01904 608700 (Visitors Booking Line)
www: www.ghosthunt.co.uk
Description: Every night – Whatever the weather – 7.30pm The Shambles. Classic York ghost stories.

York
Ghost Trail of York
Theme: Ghosts and Ghouls
Directions: 7:30pm every night from the front entrance of York Minster (West End)
Contact: Andrew Pendle
Tel: 01904 633276
Fax: 01904 640672

www: www.ghosttrail.co.uk
Disabled: All tours are wheelchair friendly.
Open:
- Daily: 7.30pm
- Closed 25th & 26th December and 1st January.
- Total duration is 1$\frac{1}{4}$ hours

Charges:
- Adult: £ 3.00
- Child: £ 2.00

Description: • Equity qualified guides • 7.30pm from the Minster (West End). Every night - whatever the weather. • Dare you travel back in time, cross the centuries and experience the stories that make up the hidden and blood chilling history of York's ghostly tradition • Traditional tales, Victorian tragedies and true accounts of modern day ghostly phenomena create a spine tingling experience that will haunt you forever.

York
Ghost Walk of York

Theme: Ghosts, Ghouls, Shock & Horror
Directions: Nightly from The King's Arms Pub, Ouse Bridge (the pub that floods) 8.00 pm.
Tel: 01759 373 090 or 01904 764 222
www: yorkshirenet.co.uk/yorkghostwalk/
Description: A favourite with clubs, societies and birthday surprises. A night of history and mystery.

York
Grand Opera House

Theme: Theatre or Playhouse
Address: Cumberland Street, York, YO1 9SW
Tel: 01904 671818
Description: Very best entertainment from West End shows to opera and ballet.

York
Haunted Walk of York

Theme: Historical Ghost Walk
Directions: Head for the City Art Gallery.
Address: 250, New Lane, Huntington, York.
Contact: Tony Mercer
Tel: 01904 621 003
E-mail: thehauntedwalkofyork@hotmail.com
Children: School parties always welcome.
Disabled: Always welcome.
Dogs: As long as they are on a leash.
Parking: In one of the many car parks in the city.
Refreshments: The local pubs and restaurants are open after the walk is finished.

Open: Every night from Easter to end of October and Friday and Saturday night all year.
Charges: Adults: £3 ● Children; £2 ● Students and Seniors £2.50
Description: The Haunted Walk is a 1hr 30min guided tour around the most haunted streets of this 2,000 year old city. ● Let our experienced guide tell you of the historic hauntings, sightings, murders and mysteries behind the most haunted city in Europe. ● No masks or gimmicks, traditional story telling: At Its Best.

York
Holy Trinity Church
Theme: Church or Church Ruins
Address: Goodramgate, York, YO1 2LF
Tel: 01904 613451
Description: York's hidden gem – a tranquil haven among the busy city streets. Much to explore.

York (Hovingham)
Hovingham Hall
Theme: House or House & Garden
Directions: Within the village
Tel: 01653 628 206
Description: Home of the Worsley Family. The Duchess of Kent is the sister of Sir Marcus Worsley. Designed in the middle 1700s by Sir Thomas Worsley.

York
Impressions Gallery
Theme: Arts Gallery or Centre
Address: 29 Castlegate, York, YO1 9RN
Tel: 01904 654724
www: www.impressions-gallery.com
Description: Changing programme of innovative contemporary photographic and new media installation work by British and international artists.

York
Jorvik Viking Centre
Theme: Visitor Centre
Directions: Situated in the Coppergate shopping area.
www: www.vikingjorvik.com
Description: The preserved remains of Jorvik have been recreated into one of the world's most enthralling reconstructions of the Viking Age.

York
McArthurGlen Designer Outlet

Theme: Shopping
Directions: At the interchange of A64 and A19 south of York, follow the signs for the Designer Outlet
Tel: 01904 682720
www: www.mcarthurglen.com
Description: Enjoy discounts of up to 50 per cent on all merchandise all day, every day. At times discounts on selected merchandise may rise to 70%.

York
Micklegate Bar Museum

Theme: Museum
Address: On the Bar Walls, York, YO1 6JX
Tel: 01904 634436
E-mail: micklegate.bar@clara.net
www: www.micklegatebar.co.uk
Shop: The Micklegate Bar Museum Shop has gifts, souvenirs and guide books for sale. Even if you're not visiting the Museum and just want to walk the City Walls then why not call in to the shop to cool down or maybe buy a present for someone at home. Maps, City Walls Walk route. Historical Scrolls, Model Soldiers, Tea Towels, CD's, Videos, Postcards, Key Rings, Ornaments, and MUCH MUCH MORE! The friendly staff are always on hand to give visitors a warm welcome, friendly advice, or directions to other attractions and places in York - so do please call in.
Open: February to October; 9am to 5pm • November to January: weekends only 9am to dusk
Charges: Adult: £2.00 • Accompanied Child: £0.50 • Concessions: £1.00
Description: Every visiting monarch and head of state has passed through this gateway, which has stood sentinel over the city for 800 years.

York
Mulberry Hall

Theme: Shopping
Speciality: Fine china, porcelain, crystal, enamels, silver and cookware.
Directions: Between York Minster and The Mansion House.
Address: Mulberry Hall, Stonegate, York, YO1 8ZW.
Tel: 01904 620 736
Fax: 01904 620 251
E-mail: mailorder@mulberryhall.co.uk
www: www.mulberryhall.co.uk
Refreshments: Mulberry Hall Coffee Shop
Open: Monday to Saturday 9am to 5.30pm

Description: Mulberry Hall on Stonegate, only 200 metres from the Minster in historic York, is one of the world's leading fine china and crystal specialists. Its beautiful timber framed building dates from 1434 and houses an unsurpassed display of the finest porcelain, crystal and homewares. The new Dining Warehouse at Mulberry Hall stocks the very best designer names for the kitchen. A delicious light lunch or afternoon tea is avalable in the Mulberry Hall Coffee Shop. If you can't visit in person then visit the Mulberry Hall website at **www.mulberryhall.co.uk** or telephone 01904 620 736.

York
National Railway Museum
Theme: Museum
Address: Leeman Road, York, YO26 4XJ
Tel: 01904 621 261
www: www.nrm.org.uk
Description: The railway story from Rocket to Eurostar. Railway artefacts include models, items of silver and crockery, nameplates, tickets, buttons posters, etc.

York
Northern Belle
Theme: Tour or Excursion
Tel: 0161 831 7900
www: www.orient-express.com
Description: 'Orient-Express of the North' is the first luxury train of the new millennium, providing enjoyable dining, day excursions and short breaks throughout the UK.

York (Nunnington)
Nunnington Hall
Theme: House & Garden
Directions: 4$\frac{1}{2}$ miles SE of Helmsley off B1257.
Tel: 01439 748 283
Description: A National Trust property. Houses the fascinating Carlisle Collection of miniature rooms fully furnished to reflect different periods. Walled garden.

York
Regimental Museum
Theme: Museum
Directions: In the centre of York opposite Clifford's Tower.
Address: Regimental Museum, 3 Tower Street, York, YO1 9SB
Tel: 01904 662790

Open:
- Daily; 9.30am to 4.30pm. except Sunday.
- Closed 22nd December to 2nd January.

Charges:
- Adult: £2.00
- Child & Senior Citizen: £1.00

Description: The Museum explores the history of two of Yorkshire's famous regiments; the Royal Dragoon Guards, and the Prince of Wale's Own Regiment of Yorkshire. With over 80 showcases housing military artefacts collected over the last 300 years. See and live the battles, courage and sacrifice made by the Yorkshire soldiers who helped to forge an empire.

York
Richard III Museum

Theme: Museum
Directions: On the City Walls at Monk Bar, 5 minutes walking distance from the City Centre. Just a stone's throw from York Minster.
Address: Monkbar, York, YO1 7LQ
Tel: 01904 634191
E-mail: info@richardiiimuseum.co.uk
www: www.richardiiimuseum.co.uk
Shop: There is an extensive Gift Shop, offering books, prints and general souvenirs. Visitors are free to browse through the Gift Shop even if the Museum does not appeal.
Open: Daily (including Sundays)
- March to October. 9am to 5pm.
- November to February. 9.30am to 4pm.
- Closed 25th & 26th December & 1st January.

Charges: Adult: £ 2.00 ● Child: £1.00 ● Child under 16: Free if accompanied by an adult. ● Senior Citizen: £ 1.00
Description: One of York's best kept secrets, housed in the tallest and most impressive of the Medieval Gatehouses. It boasts a rare example of a working portcullis, last lowered in 1953. ● The exhibition tells the story of Richard III, King of England (1483-1485). ● Presented in the form of a 'trial', the museum charges Richard with the murders of the Princes in the Tower. Visitors are invited to give their own verdict. ● The uppermost room contains the newly-added Execution Chamber, where visitors are invited (quite literally!) to re-live the executions ordered by Richard III in 1483. ● Also within Monk Bar is arguably the World's smallest Prison Cell, which held recusant Catholic Alice Bowman at the time of Elizabeth I.

York
Roam'in Tours of York

Theme : Guided Tour
Address: 18, Barney Lane, Flaxton, York, YO60 7RS
Contact: Keith Mulhearn
Tel: 07931 668 935
E-mail: keith@roamintours.co.uk
www: www.roamintours.co.uk
Children: School and children's groups are our speciality. Have a look at the comments on our web-site.
Disabled: All our tours are suitable for wheelchairs and pushchairs.
Charges: All tour prices depend on the length and number in the group.
Awards: Winner of the "City Tour of the Year" 2002. Runner-up in 2001.
Description: Walking tours around the city of York available for groups from one to "loads". ● Apart from a basic history tour we have various themed walks including Guy Fawkes, Dick Turpin, Horrid history, medieval churches, historic pub crawl, complete wall walk and the Fulford battlefield. ● Our tours are ideal for corporate occasions and can provide treasure hunts and quizes for any walk. ● We have a variety of costumed tours including Maximus Gluteus, York's resident Roman, Viking and Saxon, which are very popular with schools and cover all of the syllabus. ● We can help organise visits to other attractions and advise on accomodation and meal bookings. ● A special tour with translated leaflets is available in French, German, Italian and Spanish though we can provide a translator for a more in depth tour. ● Why not have a look at our web-site for more details and then call us with your requirements. All tours are guaranteed factual and fun.
www.roamintours.co.uk

York
St. William's College

Theme: Historic Building
Address: 4-5, College Street, York, YO1 2JF
Tel: 01904 639 347
Description: Built about 1465 for the Minster Chantry priests but after its original purpose had lapsed, it had various uses, among them that of Royal Mint and printing house for Charles I in the Civil War. It is now used for meetings but the upper floor, which has many interesting features, is open to the public.

York (Stillingfleet)
Stillingfleet Lodge Garden and Nursery
Theme: Garden or Gardens
Directions: 7 miles South of York on the B1222. Turn right just after the church, before the bridge.
Address: Stillingfleet, York, Yorkshire, YO19 6HP
Contact: Vanessa Cook
Tel: 01904 728 506
E-mail: vanessa.cook@still-lodge.freeserve.co.uk
www: www.stillingfleetlodgenurseries.co.uk
Dogs: Sorry, no dogs.
Facilities: Parking, toilets and shop on site.
Open:
- **May and June**:- Wednesday and Friday 1.00pm - 4.00pm.
- **July, August and September**:- Wednesdays 1.00pm - 4.00pm.

Charges: Adults: £2.50 • 5 to 16 yr olds: £0.50 • RHS members: admitted FREE.
Description: • Garden packed with interesting plants and foliage. Wildflower walk leading to natural pond. Long herbaceous borders and cottage garden planting round the farmhouse. • There is a National Collection of Pulmonaria (Lungwort) - a reference source of 13 species and around 150 cultivars in the garden. • Adjoining the garden there is a nursery where plants found growing in the garden may be purchased. • We specialise in unusual perennial plants, fragrant and grey foliage plants, most of which are not normally available at garden centres. • We stock a wide range of interesting plants, such as Pulmonaria (Lungwort) Geranium (Cranesbill) and Hostas, and grow a wide range of rare climbers. • As we do nearly all our own propagation, we have the knowledge to advise on what will best suit your requirements.

York
Sutton Park
Theme: House or House & Garden
Directions: 9 miles from York on B1363 to Helmsley.
Tel: 01347 810 249 or 01347 811 239
www: www.statelyhome.co.uk
Description: A fine example of early Georgian architecture filled with a rich collection of treasures. Award winning gardens. Woodland Walk

York
Theatre Royal
Theme: Theatre or Playhouse

Directions: In the Centre of York.
Tel: Box office - 01904 623 568
www: www.theatre-royal-york.co.uk
Description: City Centre theatre with shows to suit all tastes including comedy, drama, dance and musicals.

York
Treasurer's House
Theme: House & Garden
Directions: In Minster yard, just behind York Minster.
Tel: 01904 624 247
Description: A National Trust property. Was the elegant residence for Treasurers of the Minster. Peaceful walled garden in the shadow of York Minster.

York
Warner Village Cinema
Theme: Cinema or Cinema Complex
Address: Clifton Moor Centre, York, YO3 0XY
Tel: Advance bookings and programme 08702 406 020.
www: www.warnervillage.co.uk
Description: 12 screen mutliplex experience. Showing all the latest releases. Tickets may be booked on line.

York
York Barbican Centre
Theme: Concert or Music Hall
Address: Barbican Road, York, YO10 4NT
Tel: 01904 628991
Description: A varied programme of entertainments in a large concert hall, attracting top names in music.

York
York Brewery
Theme: Brewery or Brewery Visit
Directions:
- From the city centre follow Micklegate away from the city centre. Just before the city wall turn right into Toft Green.
- From the railway station turn right into Station Road. At the first set of traffic lights turn left, pass through the city wall into Micklegate and turn immediately left into Toft Green.

Address: York Brewery, 12 Toft Green, Micklegate, York, YO1 6JT
Tel: 01904 621 162
Fax: 01904 621 216
E-mail: info@yorkbrew.co.uk
www: www.yorkbrew.co.uk

Open: There is no need to book for individuals, couples or families. Just arrive at the brewery Monday to Saturday 12.30pm, 2.00pm, 3.30pm or 5.00pm Closed 25th & 26th December & 1st January.
Organised groups please book a tour by telephoning: (01904) 621 162
The perfect beginning to a social evening! Times and other details are arranged to suit your needs. Arrange your party tour by telephoning: (01904) 621 162
Charges:
- Adults £4.25
- Senior Citizens £3.75
- 14-17 years £3.00
- Free for 13 year olds and under.

Awards:
Events:
Description: York's friendly, independent Brewery, where beer is brewed using traditional methods. Join one of the guided tours for an informative and entertaining insight into the art of the master brewer. Tours include one pint of beer sampling. After the tour you can relax in the Brewery Tap Bar where the full range of beers and merchandise may be purchased. • Within the ancient walls of the City of York, beer is now being brewed commercially for the first time in forty years. The brewery brewed its first beer on May 19th 1996, and now produces a selection of top class products that have resurrected a traditional York industry. • To this end only the finest ingredients and best traditional brewing methods are being used. • York brewery was designed not only as a workplace but also as a tourist attraction. Although the general public are not allowed into the brewing areas which are kept sterile, there are specially designed viewing galleries from which the whole brewing process can be seen.

York
York City Sightseeing and Guide Friday

Theme: Guided Open Top Bus Tour
Directions: Start Point: Exhibition Square, Railway Station
Tel: 01904 65 55 85 **Fax:** 01904 65 55 87
E-mail: tlt@18rivelinway.freeserve.co.uk
www: www.city-sightseeing.com
Disabled: Wheelchairs can be accepted if folded.
Open:
- **Summer:**- Every 10 - 15 minutes every day (more frequent at peak times)
- **Winter:**- Every 30 minutes (January every hour Mon-Fri, every 30 minutes Sat & Sun)
- No tours December 24th – 26th inclusive

Charges:

- Adult: £ 7.50
  Adult fare includes 1 child (5-15 incl) free.
- Over 60 or Student: £ 5.00
- Family (2 ad+3 ch): £15.00
- Additional children (5-15) £ 3.00

Description:

The best introduction to York is to take an open top bus tour. • Hop on and off at any of our 20 stops - your ticket is valid for 24 hours.

• We offer an entertaining and informative tour, with recorded commentary in English. • Abbreviated written translations in French, German, Spanish, Italian and Japanese. For a personal touch, Guide Friday buses carry live guides in summer. • The Red route runs all year round and takes about one hour. The Green Route runs in summer, and takes about 45 minutes. Your ticket is valid on both routes. • Pay the driver on the bus. Party rates are available.

Founded in 71AD by the Romans, York has been welcoming visitors for almost 2,000 years. The City Centre is still surrounded by its mediaeval walls, and the 13th Century York Minster is the largest Gothic Cathedral in Northern Europe.

We have ancient streets and renowned museums, including the National Railway Museum, but York has managed to combine its sense of history with a thriving economy, and has some of the best shopping and entertainment around.

York
York Dungeon

Theme: Museum
Address: 12, Clifford Street, York, YO1 9RD
Tel: 01904 632 599
www: www.thedungeons.com
Description: The North's most chillingly famous horror attraction. 2,000 years of gruesomely authentic history.

York (Rufforth)
York Gliding Centre

Theme: Sport
Address: The Aerodrome, Rufforth, York, YO23 3NA
Tel: 01904 738 694
Description: Look down on the magnificence of the city of York and the beautiful Vale of York that surrounds it.

York
York Maize Maze
Theme: Maze

Directions: Located close to York adjoining the Grimston Bar Park and Ride Site. ● Take the A64 to the York Bypass and turn into York where the A1079 meets the Bypass and follow the signs into Grimston Bar Park and Ride. ● The Maze will be signed within the site. ● Alternatively; use the bus service from the city centre which takes you directly to the Park and Ride. ● Journey time is about 10 minutes.

Address: Botland Farm, Heslington, York, YO10 5EG

Tel: 01904 415 364

Fax: 01904 427 829

www: www.yorkmaze.co.uk

Disabled: Suitable as long as you avoid wet weather.

Dogs: Welcome on a lead.

Parking: FREE.

Toilets: At Park and Ride (100 yds)

Refreshments: Refreshment & Picnic Area available.

Open: Throughout August and September ● 10am to 5pm every day

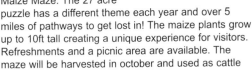

Charges:

Adult: £3.50

Child: £2.50

Under 5s: FREE

Description: The UK's largest Maize Maze. The 27 acre puzzle has a different theme each year and over 5 miles of pathways to get lost in! The maize plants grow up to 10ft tall creating a unique experience for visitors. Refreshments and a picnic area are available. The maze will be harvested in october and used as cattle feed for the winter. Follow the signs for the Grimston Bar Park & Ride, or catch the bus from the city centre.

York
York Minster

Theme : Cathedral or Cathedral Ruins
Directions: Well signed within the City
Tel: 01904 557 216
www: www.yorkminster.org
Description: The chief church in the Northern Province of the Church of England. Seat of the Archbishop of York. Largest medieval cathedral in Northern Europe. The first minster was 7th century; the present one is the fourth on the site. Archbishop de Grey began the great building about 1220, it was completed in 1472.

York
York Model Railway

Theme: Miniature or Model Railway
Address: Tea Room Square, York Station, YO24 1AY
Tel: 01904 630 169
E-mail: ymr@compuserve.com
Disabled: Wheelchair access and all on ground floor.
Dogs: Guide dogs only please.
Parking: Nearby public parking.
Toilets: Available on station.
Shop: Models and gifts available.
Open: March to October 9am-6pm. • November to February 10am-5pm. • Last admissions half hour before closing. • Closed 25th and 26th December
Charges: Adult: £3.40 • Child: £2.00 • Family: £9.50 • Student: £2.80 • Concession: Special rates for group visits can be pre-arranged in or out of normal opening times • Senior Citizen: £2.80
Description: This little exhibition is easily missed in its spot beside the Railway Station but it is in an ideal place for miniature railway enthusiasts in particular, and fun for adults and children alike, with approximately 330 metres of track making up four main routes on the "00" gauge layout. • Up to 21 trains operate at the same time. These comprise HST 125's and a variety of other freight and passenger trains including steam, diesel and electric trains. • Thousands of miniature detail features such as trees, bushes, vehicles, figures and buildings add to the realism of the display. • Everyone can join in the fun by pushing the interactive buttons throughout. • There is a separate Thomas the Tank area designed for the younger children. • Plus an alpine "N" gauge display with day to night lighting features.

York
York Shakespeare Project

Theme: Theatre or Playhouse
Tel: 01904 647 537
E-mail: eileen@yorkshakespeare.org.uk
www: www.yorkshakespeare.org.uk
Events: 2003

- Taming of the Shrew – Ring to confirm all dates
  13th and 14th June – Pocklington Civic Arts Centre.
  Week beginning 15th June – Joseph Rowntree
  Theatre.
- Comedy of Errors – Ring to confirm all dates
  Week beginning 10th November – Friargate
  Theatre
  20th November – Burton Stone Lane C.C.
  21st November – Tang Hall C.C.
  22nd November – Foxwood C.C.

Description: Made up of both amateur and professional actors and producers/directors who intend to produce all of Shakespeare's 37 plays in York over the next 20 years. Plays are due to be staged at venues throughout the city.

York
YorkBoat

Theme: Boat Hire or Cruise
Address: Office at The Boatyard, Lendal Bridge, York, YO1 7DP
Tel: 01904 628 324
Fax: 01904 647 204
E-mail: info@yorkboat.co.uk
www: www.yorkboat.co.uk
Open: Regular daytime sailings from city centre landings from 10.30am, 8th February to 23rd November 2003. Ghost Cruises at 7pm from Kings Staith, Floodlit Evening Cruises at 9.15pm from Lendal Bridge, every night 29th March to 1st November 2003.
Awards: Quality Assured Visitor Attraction, ETC.
Description: Make the most of your day and enjoy the

sights of York city and country from onboard a **GUIDED RIVER TRIP** with captain's commentary or take the helm of your own **REDBOAT** self drive motor boat.

For an evening with a difference join the 'spirits' at the bar on the **GHOST CRUISE** with an entertaining storyteller. Or relax onboard the **FLOODLIT EVENING CRUISE** to Bishopthorpe Palace

Or why not join a **THEMED PARTY CRUISE** during the summer! Every YorkBoat has modern toilets, heated lounges with panoramic windows, tea/coffee and bar facilities and open sundecks!

York (Elvington)
Yorkshire Air Museum
Theme: Museum (Air)
Address: Halifax Way, Elvington, York, YO1 4AU
Tel: 01904 608 595 **Fax:** 01904 608 246
Description: Includes the last Handley-Page Halifax bomber and a collection dedicated to Barnes Wallis who devised the bouncing "dambuster" bomb in 1943.

York
Yorkshire Lavender
Theme: Garden or Gardens (Lavender products)
Address: Terrington, York, YO6O 6PP
Tel: 01653 648 008
www: www.lavenderworld.com
Description: Will thrive in most soil and climate conditions and is a beautiful and fragrant plant to have.

York
Yorkshire Museum of Farming
Theme: Museum
Address: Murton Park, Murton Lane, York, Y019 5UF
Tel: 01904 489966
www: www murtonpark.co.uk
Description: Farm implements and machinery ●
Derwent Valley Light Railway ● Danelaw Replica Dark Age village. ● Brigantium - Replica Roman Fort ● etc

York
Yorkwalk
Theme: Guided Walk or Tour
Address: Yorkwalk, 3, Fairway, York, YO30 5QA
Tel: 01904 622 303
Fax: 01904 656 244
E-mail: admin@yorkwalk.fsnet.co.uk
www: www.yorkwalk.co.uk

Disabled: Most walks wheelchair accessible.
Dogs: Welcome on many walks.
Parking: Marygate Car Park.
Toilets: Yes.
Refreshments: Yes.
Open: 10:30am and 2:15pm daily from February to November • Weekends only December and January. Walks start at the Museum Gardens Gates on Museum Street, just north of Lendal Bridge.
Charges:

- Adult: £5.00
- Accompanied Child (6 – 15):   £2.00
- Child (under 6):   Free
- Disabled, Students, YHA and
  Yorkcard holders, .   £4.50

Description: Reach the parts of York other visitors miss! Entertaining Historical Guided Walks. Qualified guides inform and entertain you as they personally conduct you around the ancient city of York. Special themed walks include Historic Toilet Tour, Inaccessible York and Graveyard Tours. Private bookings welcome at any time. Please ring or visit **www.yorkwalk.co.uk** for more details.

York
Yorvik Brass Rubbing Centre

Theme: Brass Rubbing
Directions: In the gardens of Lady Anne Middleton's Hotel, Skeldergate. 5 minutes walk from the city centre over the Ouse or Skeldergate bridges.
Tel: 01904 630 456 Ext: 226
E-mail: brass@rubbings.fsnet.co.uk
www: www.brass-rubbing.com
Children: Very suitable for children.
Shop: Jewellery, gifts, information, sweets.
Open: All year. Daily 10am - 5pm.
Closed: Sundays October to March.
Charges: Admission is FREE. £3.50 per rubbing.

Description: The collection of Medieval and Tudor brass facsimilies are available for visitors to make rubbings, with all the specialist materials and friendly instruction on brass rubbing techniques.

PLACES OF INTEREST

You may search this INDEX by
Place Name, by Town or by Theme

PLACES OF INTEREST

PLACES OF INTEREST

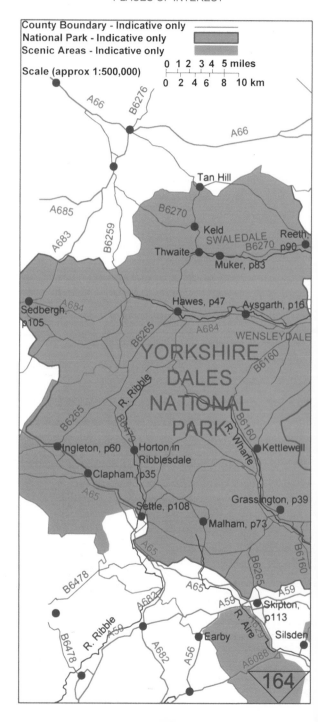

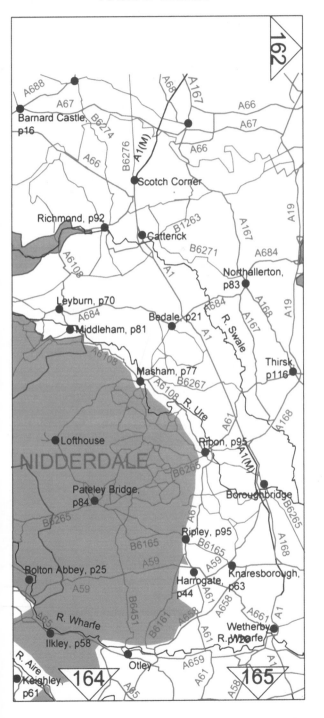

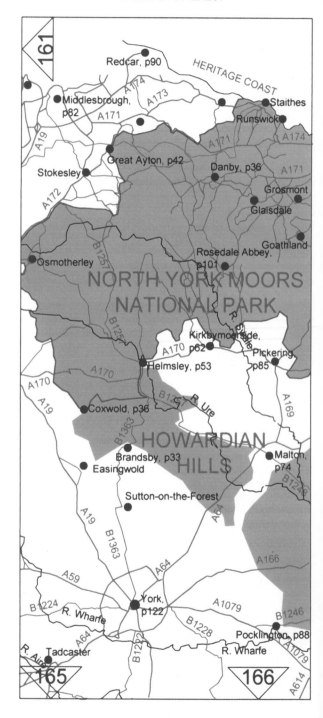

PLACES OF INTEREST

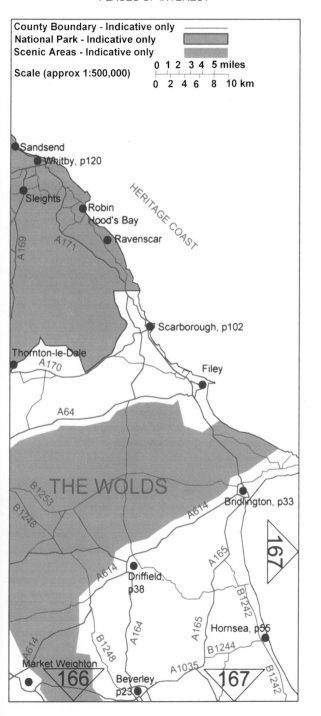

County Boundary - Indicative only
National Park - Indicative only
Scenic Areas - Indicative only

Scale (approx 1:500,000)

0 1 2 3 4 5 miles
0 2 4 6 8 10 km

Sandsend
Whitby, p120
Sleights
A169
A171
HERITAGE COAST
Robin Hood's Bay
Ravenscar
Scarborough, p102
Thornton-le-Dale
A170
Filey
A64
THE WOLDS
B1253
B1248
Bridlington, p33
A614
A165
167
A614
Driffield, p38
A164
A165
B1242
Hornsea, p55
B1244
A614
B1248
A1035
A1035
Market Weighton
166
Beverley, p23
167
B1242

PLACES OF INTEREST

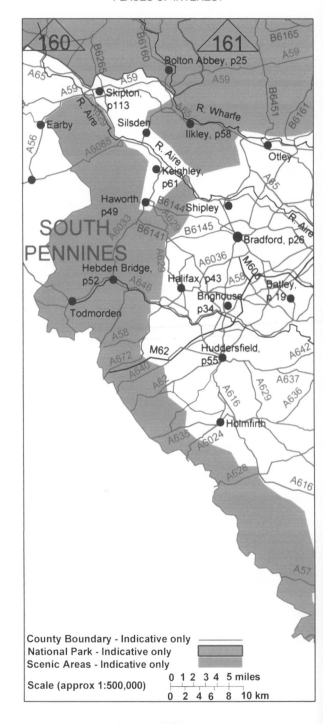

160

161

Bolton Abbey, p25

Skipton, p113

R. Wharfe

A59

Earby

Silsden

R. Aire

Ilkley, p58

Otley

Keighley, p61

Haworth, p49

Shipley

SOUTH
PENNINES

Bradford, p26

Hebden Bridge, p52

Halifax, p43

Brighouse, p34

Batley, p19

Todmorden

Huddersfield, p55

M62

Holmfirth

County Boundary - Indicative only
National Park - Indicative only
Scenic Areas - Indicative only

Scale (approx 1:500,000)

0 1 2 3 4 5 miles
0 2 4 6 8 10 km

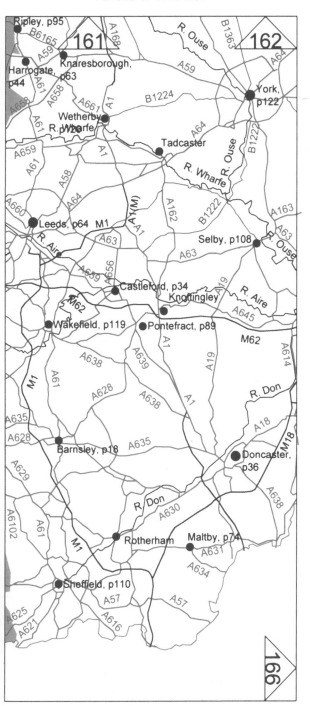

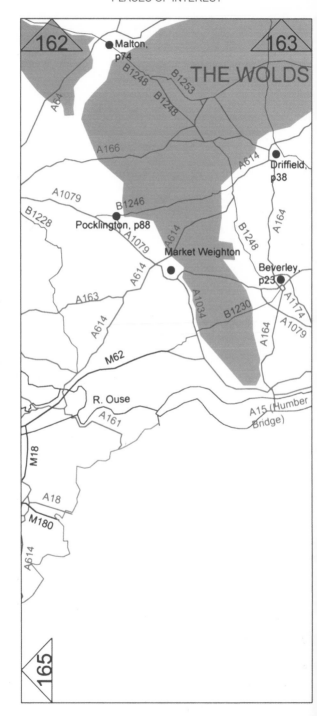

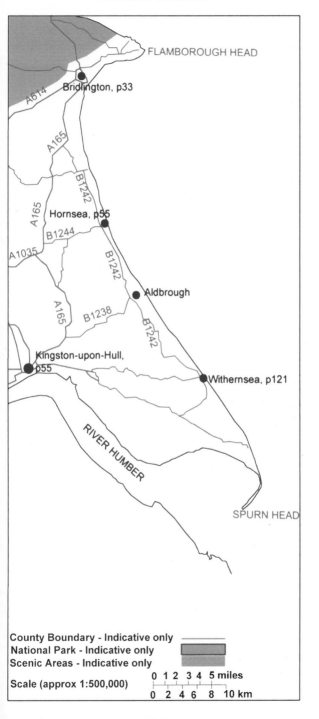

PLACES OF INTEREST

Visitor's Notes